Houghton
Mifflin
Harcourt

CALIFORNIA

MATH

Expressions
Common Core

Dr. Karen C. Fuson

GRADE

K

Volume 2

This material is based upon work supported by the
National Science Foundation
under Grant Numbers
ESI-9816320, REC-9806020, and RED-935373.

Any opinions, findings, and conclusions, or recommendations expressed in this material
are those of the author and do not necessarily reflect the views of the National Science Foundation.

Printed in the U.S.A.

ISBN: 978-0-544-20403-4

5 6 7 8 9 10   1421   23 22 21 20 19 18 17 16 15 14

4500489251   B C D E F G

VOLUME 2 CONTENTS

UNIT 4 Partners, Problem Drawings, and Tens

BIG IDEA I	Story Problems and Equations

BIG IDEA 2	Practice with Comparing

© Houghton Mifflin Harcourt Publishing Company

* This lesson consists only of activities from the Teacher Edition.

VOLUME 2 CONTENTS *(continued)*

* This lesson consists only of activities from the Teacher Edition.

UNIT 5 Consolidation of Concepts

© Houghton Mifflin Harcourt Publishing Company

VOLUME 2 CONTENTS (continued)

* This lesson consists only of activities from the Teacher Edition.

© Houghton Mifflin Harcourt Publishing Company

Dear Family:

Ask your child about our pretend grocery store at school! Children will be using the groceries from this pretend store to create addition and subtraction story problems, such as the following:

There are 3 bananas in this bunch and 4 bananas in the other bunch. How many bananas are there in all?

You and your child can create similar story problems with groceries in your own kitchen. When doing so, you may need to help your child say the question at the end of the story problem.

Addition example:
There are 5 cans on the top shelf. There are 4 cans on the bottom shelf. How many cans are there?

Subtraction example:
There are 10 eggs in the carton. If we cook 3 eggs, how many eggs are left in the carton?

It is not necessary to solve all of the story problems. Learning to visualize the situation and state the story problem are both important tasks, even without solving. Asking questions different ways is also helpful.

Have fun!

Sincerely,
Your child's teacher

CA CC

Unit 4 addresses the following standards from the *Common Core State Standards for Mathematics with California Additions*: K.CC.1, K.CC.3, K.CC.4, K.CC.4a, K.CC.4b, K.CC.4c, K.CC.5, K.CC.6, K.CC.7, K.OA.1, K.OA.2, K.OA.3, K.OA.4, K.OA.5, K.NBT.1, K.MD.3, K.G.1, K.G.2, K.G.3, K.G.4, K.G.5, K.G.6 and all Mathematical Practices.

Estimada familia:

¡Pregunte a su niño por la tiendita que tenemos en la escuela! Los niños van a usar los comestibles de la tiendita para crear problemas de suma y resta, como los siguientes:

Hay 3 plátanos en este racimo y 4 plátanos en el otro. ¿Cuántos plátanos hay en total?

Usted y su niño pueden formular problemas parecidos con los comestibles que tengan en su cocina. Al hacerlo, tal vez tenga que ayudar a su niño a formular la pregunta del final del problema.

Ejemplo de suma:
Hay 5 latas en el estante superior. Hay 4 latas en el estante inferior. ¿Cuántas latas hay?

Ejemplo de resta:
Hay 10 huevos en la caja. Si usamos 3 huevos, ¿cuántos huevos quedan en la caja?

No es necesario resolver todos los problemas. Aprender a visualizar la situación y a formular el problema son destrezas importantes, aun si los problemas no se resuelven. Formular preguntas de distintas maneras también es de mucha ayuda.

¡Que se diviertan!

Atentamente,
El maestro de su niño

CA CC

En la Unidad 4 se aplican los siguientes estándares auxiliares, contenidos en los *Estándares Estatales Comunes de Matemáticas con Adiciones para California*: **K.CC.1, K.CC.3, K.CC.4, K.CC.4a, K.CC.4b, K.CC.4c, K.CC.5, K.CC.6, K.CC.7, K.OA.1, K.OA.2, K.OA.3, K.OA.4, K.OA.5, K.NBT.1, K.MD.3, K.G.1, K.G.2, K.G.3, K.G.4, K.G.5, K.G.6** y todos los de prácticas matemáticas.

Name

Puzzled Penguin counted the cherries.

Look at what Puzzled Penguin wrote.

Help Puzzled Penguin.

14 cherries

Am I correct?

_____ cherries

Numbers 1–10 and Math Stories: Grocery Store Scenario

Cut on the dashed lines.

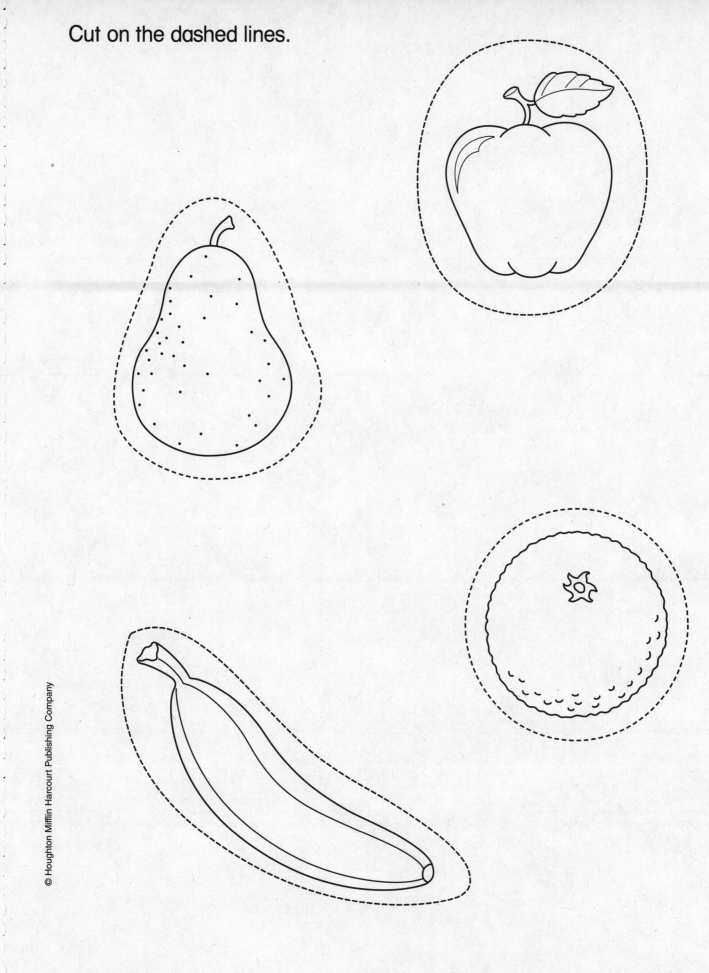

Fruit

Cut on the dashed lines.

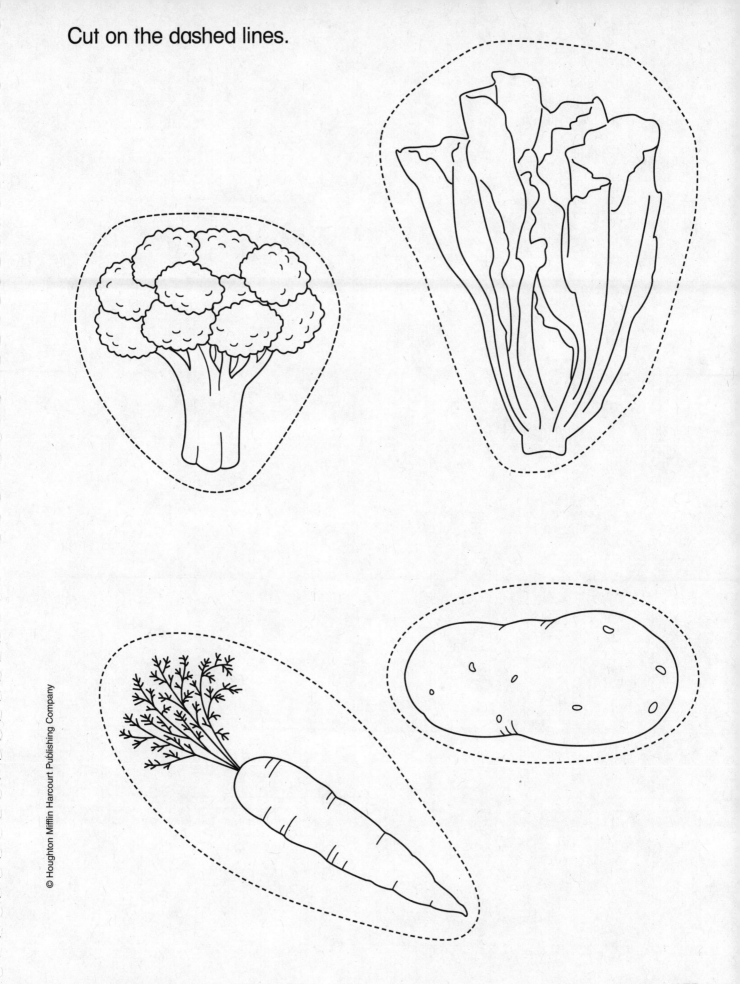

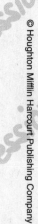

Vegetables

Name

CA CC Content Standards **K.OA.3, K.OA.4**
Mathematical Practices **MP.7**

I. Draw a line to show the **partners**. Then write the partners.

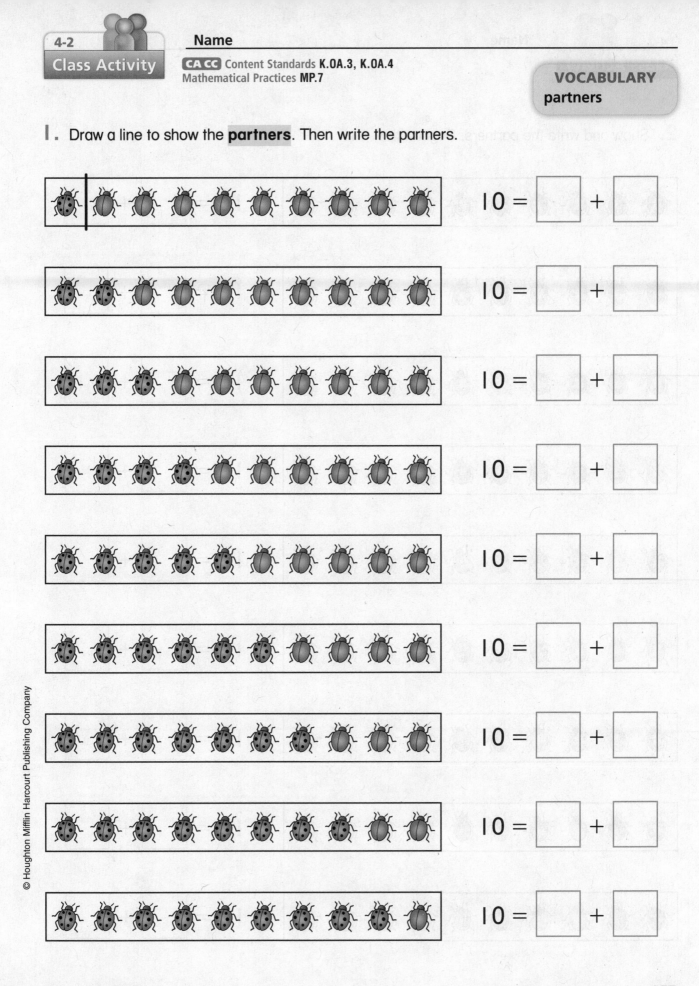

10 = ☐ + ☐

10 = ☐ + ☐

10 = ☐ + ☐

10 = ☐ + ☐

10 = ☐ + ☐

10 = ☐ + ☐

10 = ☐ + ☐

10 = ☐ + ☐

10 = ☐ + ☐

Find Partners of 10 **157**

Name _____

2. Show and write the partners. Begin with 9 + 1.

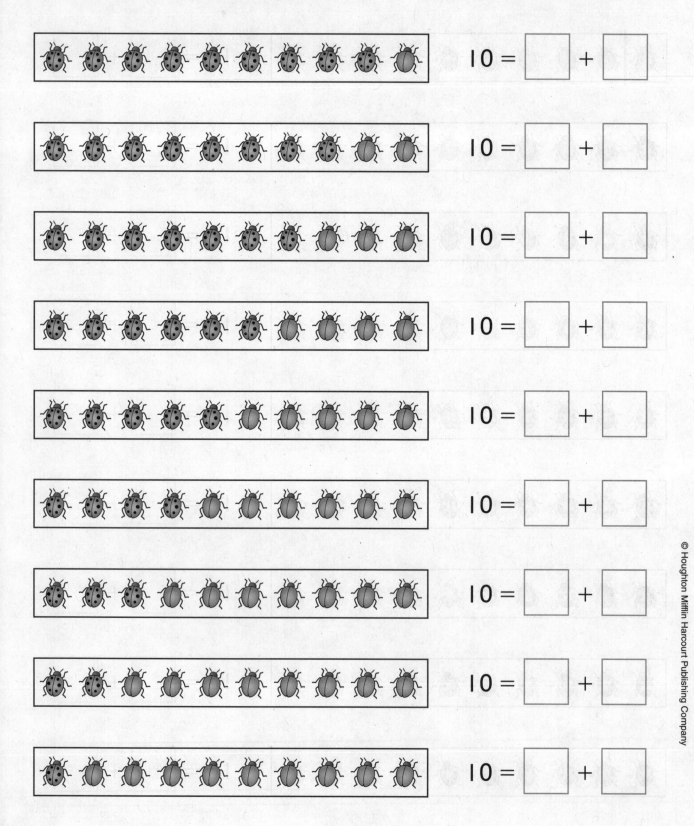

$$10 = \boxed{} + \boxed{}$$

$$10 = \boxed{} + \boxed{}$$

$$10 = \boxed{} + \boxed{}$$

$$10 = \boxed{} + \boxed{}$$

$$10 = \boxed{} + \boxed{}$$

$$10 = \boxed{} + \boxed{}$$

$$10 = \boxed{} + \boxed{}$$

$$10 = \boxed{} + \boxed{}$$

$$10 = \boxed{} + \boxed{}$$

Find Partners of 10

Set A

$11 = 10 + 1$	$12 = 10 + 2$	$13 = 10 + 3$	$14 = 10 + 4$	$15 = 10 + 5$
$16 = 10 + 6$	$17 = 10 + 7$	$18 = 10 + 8$	$19 = 10 + 9$	$20 = 10 + 10$

Set B

$10 + 1 = 11$	$10 + 2 = 12$	$10 + 3 = 13$	$10 + 4 = 14$	$10 + 5 = 15$
$10 + 6 = 16$	$10 + 7 = 17$	$10 + 8 = 18$	$10 + 9 = 19$	$10 + 10 = 20$

Teen Equation Cards

Teen Equation Cards

Name

CA CC Content Standards **K.CC.3, K.OA.1, K.OA.5, K.NBT.1**
Mathematical Practices **MP.1**

1. Show the partners with fingers. Then write the total.

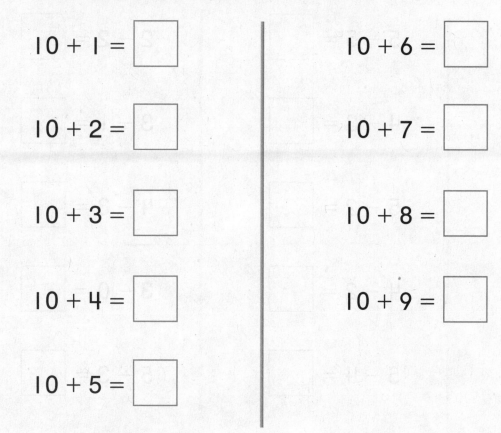

$10 + 1 = \boxed{}$ $10 + 6 = \boxed{}$

$10 + 2 = \boxed{}$ $10 + 7 = \boxed{}$

$10 + 3 = \boxed{}$ $10 + 8 = \boxed{}$

$10 + 4 = \boxed{}$ $10 + 9 = \boxed{}$

$10 + 5 = \boxed{}$

2. Write the numbers 1–20.

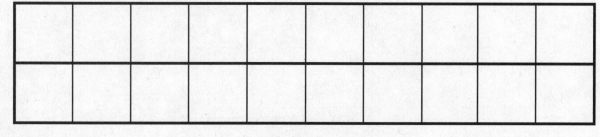

3. Draw a picture to show 10 ones and 2 ones.

PATH to
FLUENCY

4. Subtract the numbers. Use your fingers or draw.

$3 - 2 = \boxed{}$ $5 - 5 = \boxed{}$ $2 - 2 = \boxed{}$

$4 - 1 = \boxed{}$ $4 - 3 = \boxed{}$ $3 - 1 = \boxed{}$

$3 - 3 = \boxed{}$ $5 - 2 = \boxed{}$ $4 - 3 = \boxed{}$

$5 - 0 = \boxed{}$ $4 - 2 = \boxed{}$ $3 - 0 = \boxed{}$

$2 - 1 = \boxed{}$ $5 - 4 = \boxed{}$ $5 - 3 = \boxed{}$

5. Choose an equation. Draw a picture to show the subtraction. Write the equation.

Teen Numbers and Equations

Family Letter

Content Overview

Dear Family:

Throughout the year, your child will be learning how to "break apart" numbers. For example, 6 equals 5 and 1, 4 and 2, and 3 and 3. We call two numbers that add up to a number the *partners* of the number.

To strengthen your child's understanding of these concepts, you can play *The Unknown Partner Game* with him or her. The game is played as follows:

Put out 5 objects such as buttons or crackers. Count them together. Have your child cover his or her eyes while you take a partner away. Ask your child to tell you the missing amount. Now it is your turn to close your eyes!

You can play this game again and again, starting with a different total each time. Start with 5 first (because it is easiest), and then move on to 6, 7, 8, 9, and 10.

Thank you!

Sincerely,
Your child's teacher

CA CC

Unit 4 addresses the following standards from the *Common Core State Standards for Mathematics with California Additions*: K.CC.1, K.CC.3, K.CC.4, K.CC.4a, K.CC.4b, K.CC.4c, K.CC.5, K.CC.6, K.CC.7, K.OA.1, K.OA.2, K.OA.3, K.OA.4, K.OA.5, K.NBT.1, K.MD.3, K.G.1, K.G.2, K.G.3, K.G.4, K.G.5, K.G.6 and all Mathematical Practices.

Estimada familia:

Durante todo el año su niño aprenderá a "separar" números. Por ejemplo, 6 es igual a 5 más 1, 4 más 2, y 3 más 3. A dos números que sumados dan como resultado otro número los llamamos *partes* del número.

Puede jugar al juego de las partes desconocidas con su niño para reforzar estas ideas. Se juega de esta manera:

Coloque en algún lugar 5 objetos, como botones o galletas. Cuéntenlos juntos. Pida a su niño que se tape los ojos mientras Ud. quita una parte. Pida a su niño que diga la cantidad que falta. ¡Ahora es su turno de cerrar los ojos!

Jueguen varias veces, siempre empezando con un total diferente. Empiecen con 5 (por ser el más fácil) y sigan con 6, 7, 8, 9 y 10.

¡Gracias!

Atentamente,
El maestro de su niño

 CA CC

En la Unidad 4 se aplican los siguientes estándares auxiliares, contenidos en los *Estándares Estatales Comunes de Matemáticas con Adiciones para California*: **K.CC.1, K.CC.3, K.CC.4, K.CC.4a, K.CC.4b, K.CC.4c, K.CC.5, K.CC.6, K.CC.7, K.OA.1, K.OA.2, K.OA.3, K.OA.4, K.OA.5, K.NBT.1, K.MD.3, K.G.1, K.G.2, K.G.3, K.G.4, K.G.5, K.G.6** y todos los de prácticas matemáticas.

Class Activity

Name _____

CA CC Content Standards **K.CC.4, K.CC.5, K.CC.6, K.CC.7** Mathematical Practices **MP.2, MP.7, MP.8**

VOCABULARY
extra
greater
less

Draw lines to match. Circle the **extras**.

Write the numbers and compare them.

Write G for **Greater** and L for **Less**.

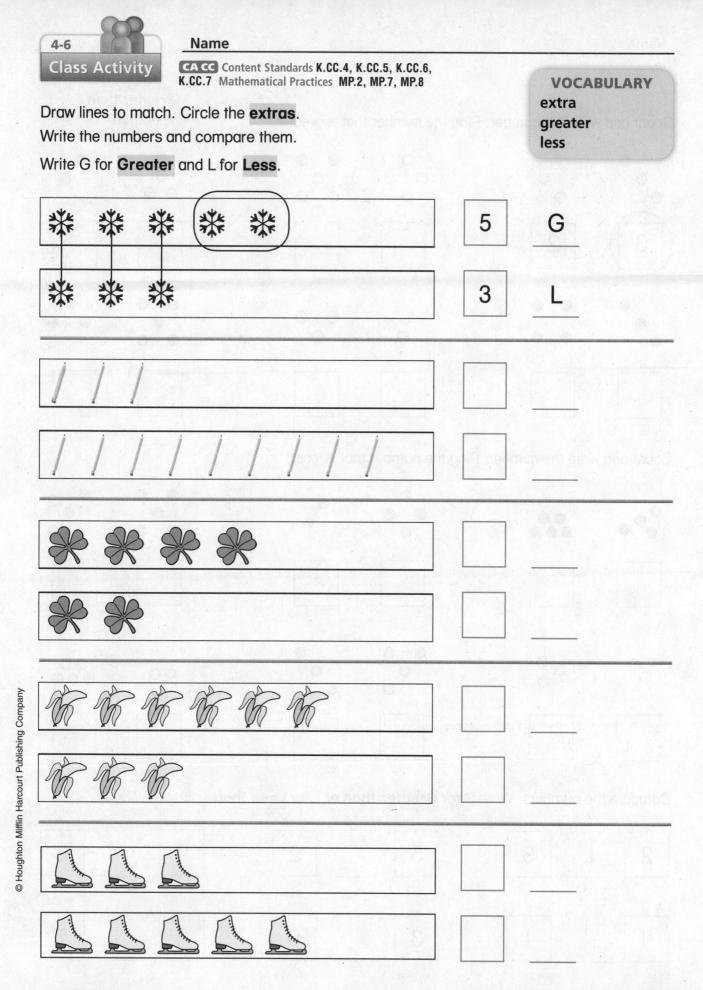

Count, Match, and Compare **165**

VOCABULARY
greater than
less than

Count and write the number. Ring the number that is greater.

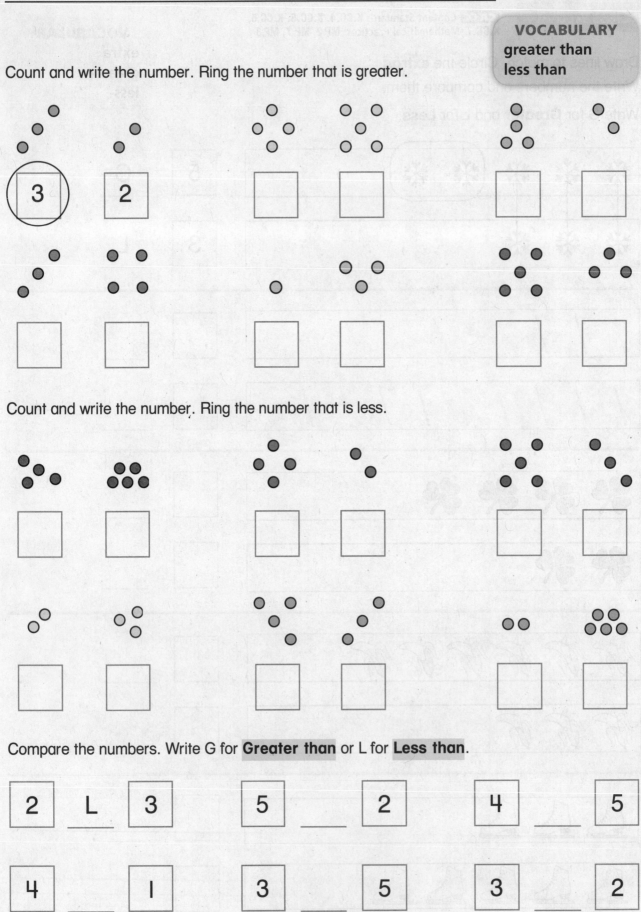

Count and write the number. Ring the number that is less.

Compare the numbers. Write G for **Greater than** or L for **Less than**.

| 2 | L | 3 | | 5 | | 2 | | 4 | | 5 |

| 4 | | 1 | | 3 | | 5 | | 3 | | 2 |

Count, Match, and Compare

Name _____

CA CC Content Standards K.CC.3, K.CC.5, K.OA.3, K.OA.4
Mathematical Practices MP.4, MP.7

Draw a line to show two **partners**. Write the partners.

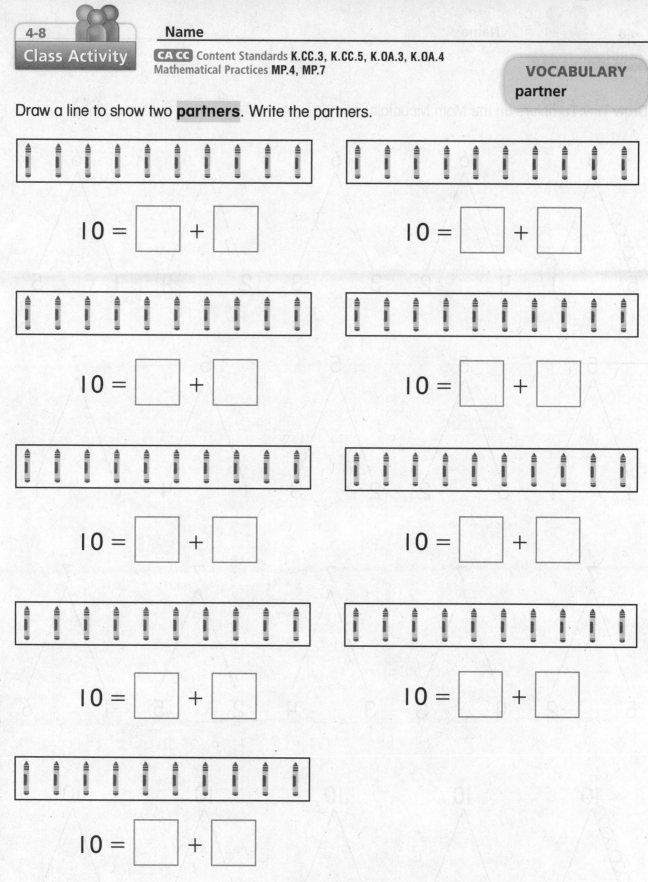

10 = ☐ + ☐

10 = ☐ + ☐

10 = ☐ + ☐

10 = ☐ + ☐

10 = ☐ + ☐

10 = ☐ + ☐

10 = ☐ + ☐

10 = ☐ + ☐

10 = ☐ + ☐

Draw Tiny Tumblers on the Math Mountains.

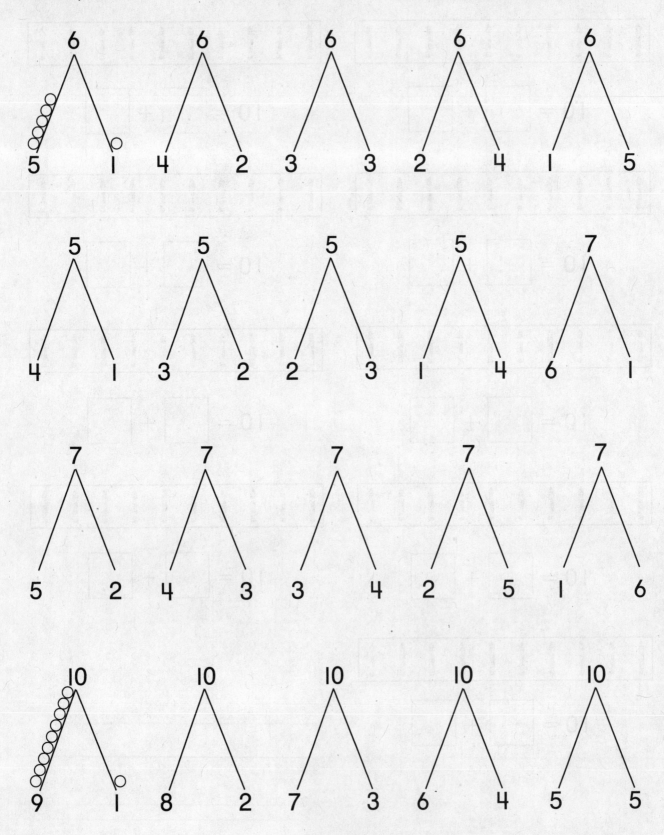

Break-Apart Numbers for 10

Write the numbers 1 through 20 in order.

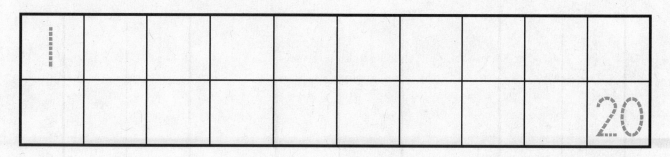

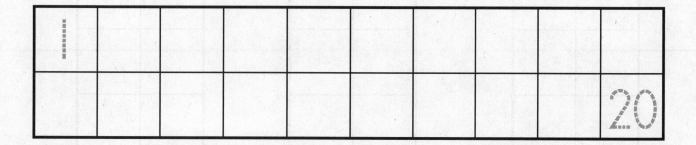

Count how many. Write the number.

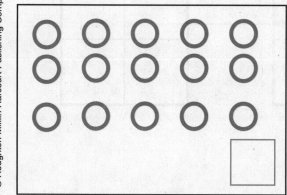

Write the numbers 1 through 20 in order.

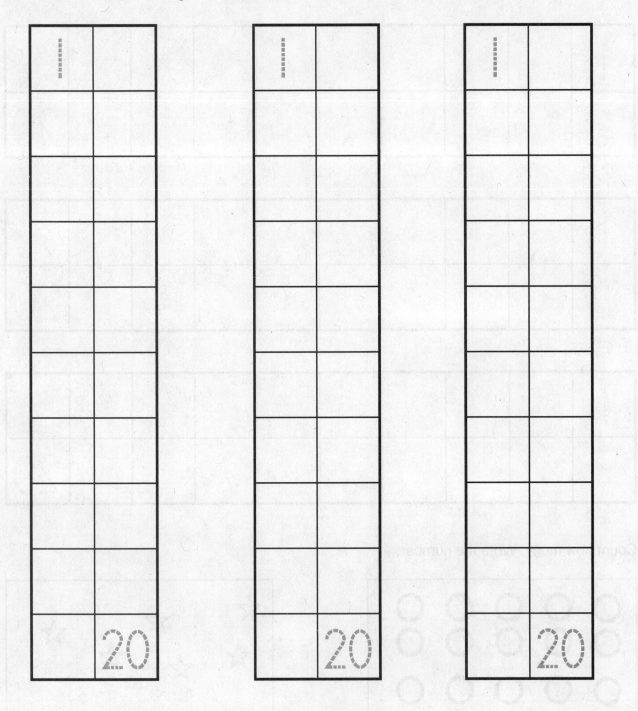

Break-Apart Numbers for 10

Name _____

CA CC Content Standards **K.MD.3, K.G.2, K.G.3, K.G.4**
Mathematical Practices **MP.1, MP.3, MP.6**

1. Look at each shape. Write the number of straight sides.

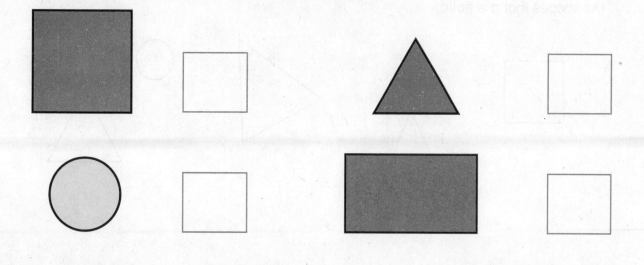

2. Look at each shape. Write the number of corners.

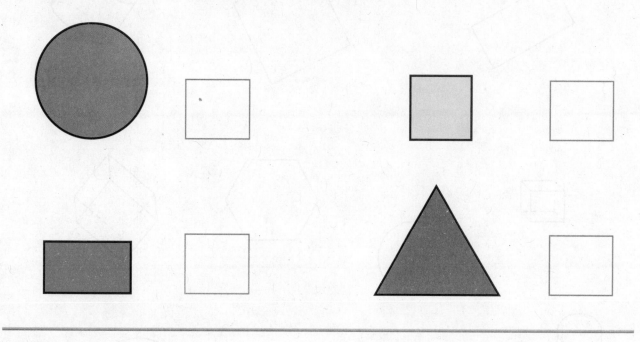

3. Ring the shape that has 4 sides of equal length.

VOCABULARY
flat
solid

4. Look at each shape. Ring the shapes that are **flat**. Mark an X on the shapes that are **solid**.

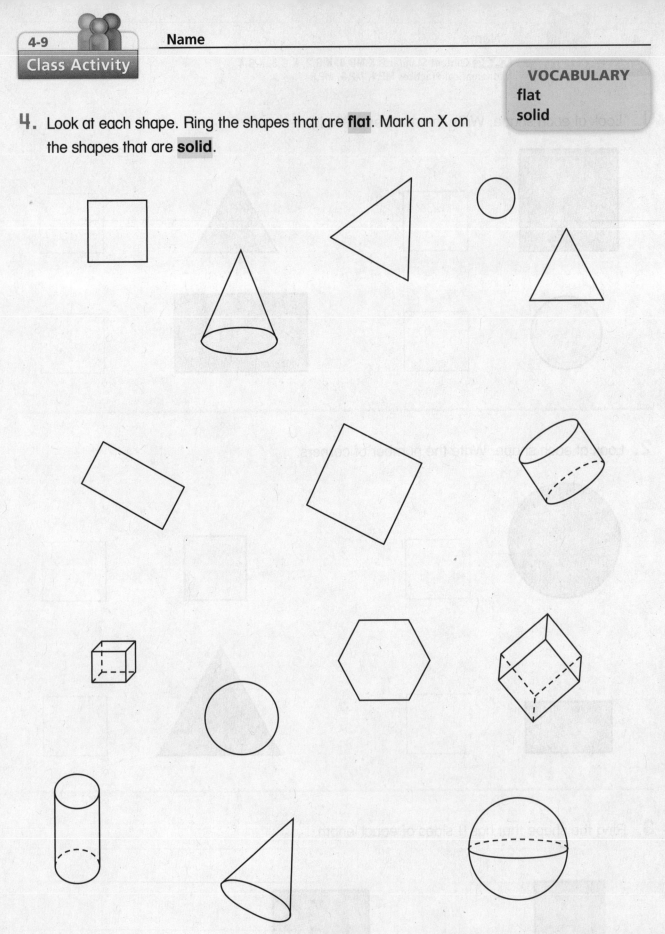

Attributes of 3-Dimensional Shapes

Name _____

CA CC Content Standards **K.CC.3, K.CC.6, K.CC.7**
Mathematical Practices **MP.6**

1. Count and write the number. Ring the number that is **greater**.

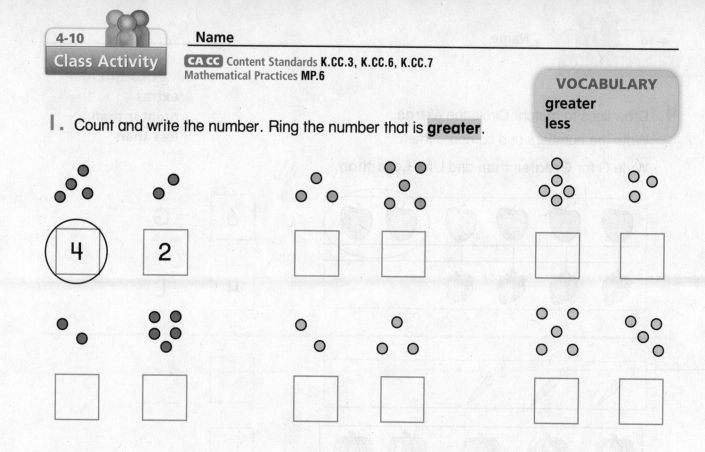

2. Count and write the number. Ring the number that is **less**.

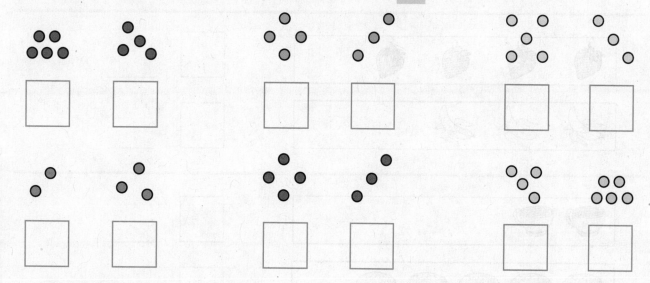

3. Write the numbers 1 through 20 in order.

VOCABULARY
extras
greater than
less than

4. Draw lines to match. Circle the **extras**.

Write the numbers and compare them.

Write G for **Greater than** and L for **Less than**.

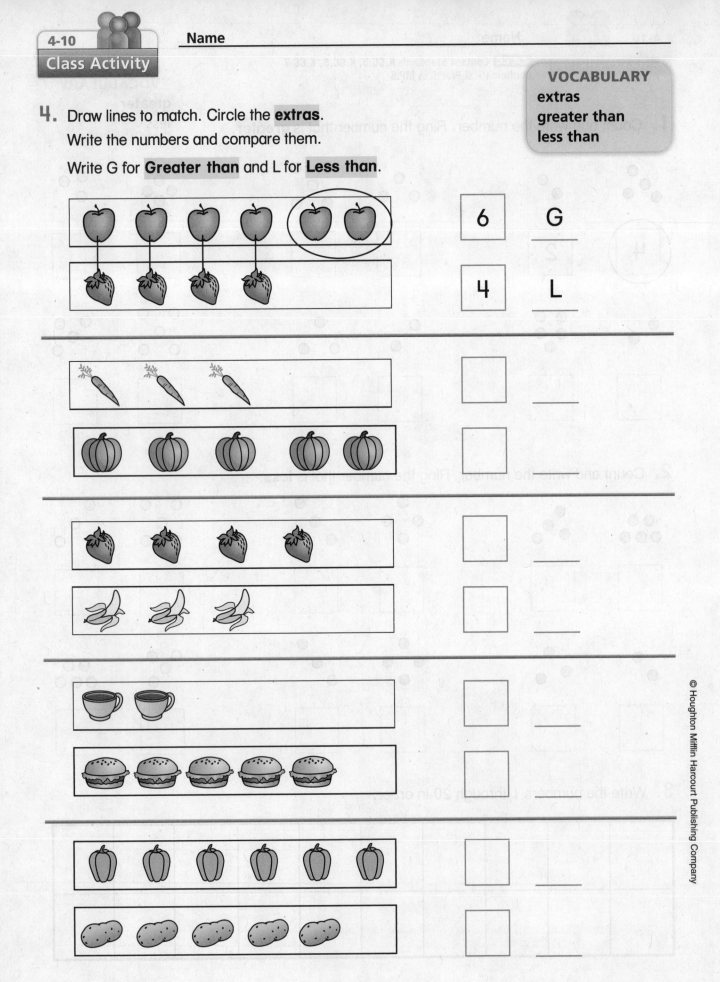

Addition and Subtraction Drawings: Grocery Store Scenario

VOCABULARY
partners

1. Draw a line to show the **partners**. Write the partners.

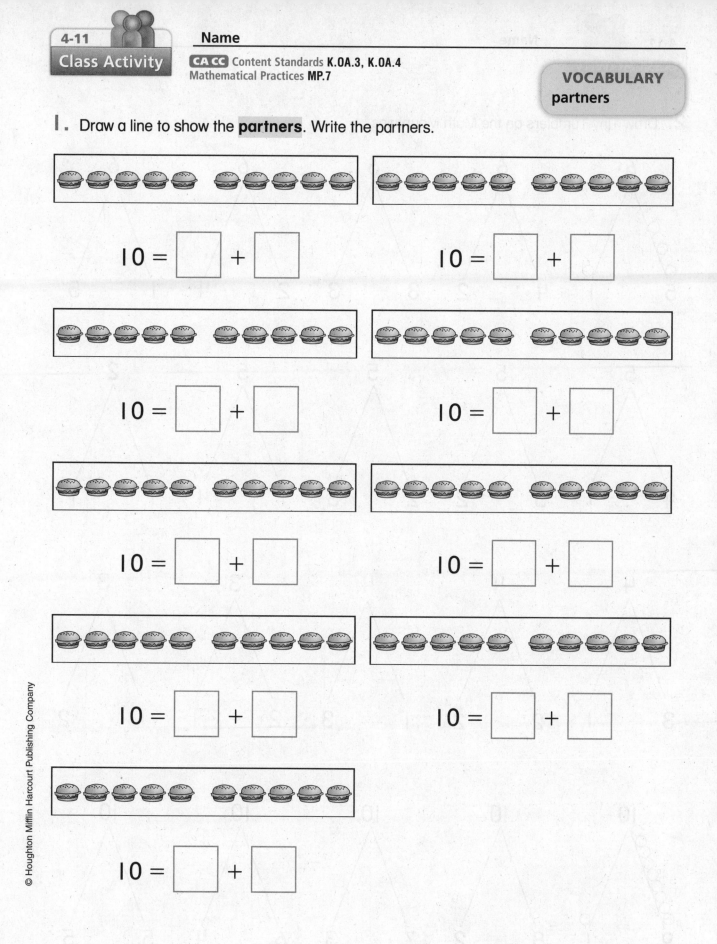

10 = ☐ + ☐   10 = ☐ + ☐

10 = ☐ + ☐   10 = ☐ + ☐

10 = ☐ + ☐   10 = ☐ + ☐

10 = ☐ + ☐   10 = ☐ + ☐

10 = ☐ + ☐

© Houghton Mifflin Harcourt Publishing Company

2. Draw Tiny Tumblers on the Math Mountains.

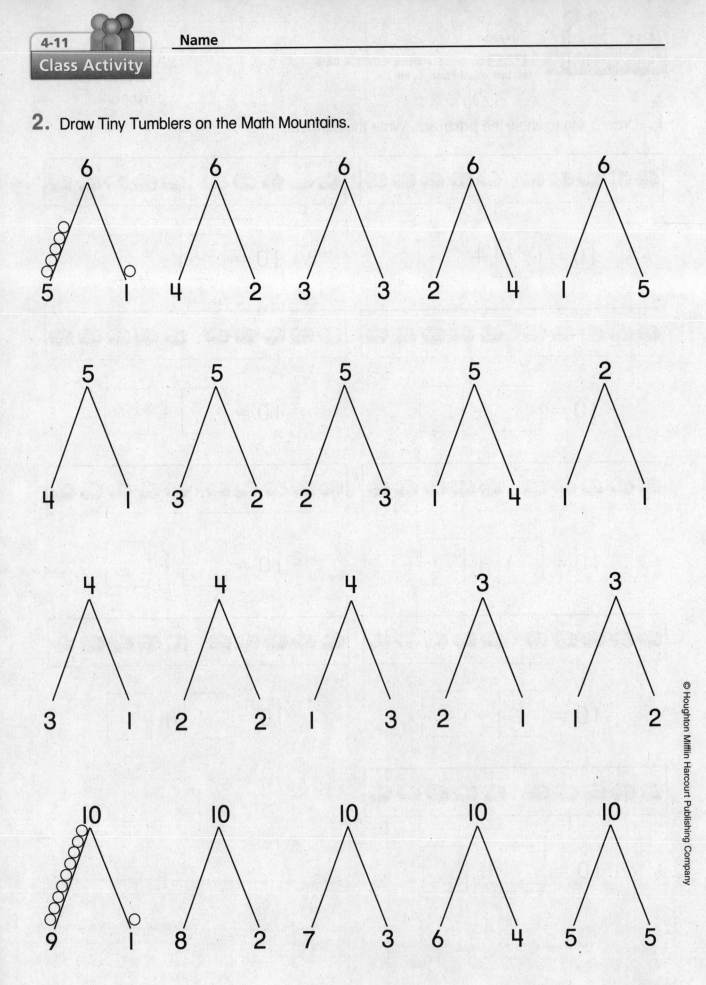

Partners of 10 with 5-Groups

Family Letter

Content Overview

Dear Family:

In your child's math program, partners are numbers that go together to make up another number. For example:

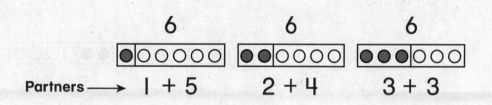

Partners ⟶ 1 + 5   2 + 4   3 + 3

Knowing partners of numbers will help your child develop a strong sense of relationships among numbers and provide a firm foundation for learning addition and subtraction.

Your child has begun using "Math Mountain" drawings to show partners of numbers. Children were told a story about "Tiny Tumblers" who live on top of "Math Mountain." These Tiny Tumblers roll down the sides of Math Mountain for fun. For example:

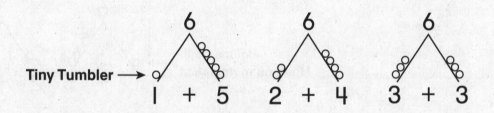

Tiny Tumbler ⟶ 1 + 5   2 + 4   3 + 3

Your child will be asked to count Tiny Tumblers (small circles like those above) and draw Tiny Tumblers to show partners. Children enjoy this visual support and can more easily internalize partners with continued practice. Please help your child with Math Mountain pages as necessary.

Thank you!

Sincerely,
Your child's teacher

© Houghton Mifflin Harcourt Publishing Company

 CA CC

Unit 4 addresses the following standards from the *Common Core State Standards for Mathematics with California Additions*: **K.CC.1, K.CC.3, K.CC.4, K.CC.4a, K.CC.4b, K.CC.4c, K.CC.5, K.CC.6, K.CC.7, K.OA.1, K.OA.2, K.OA.3, K.OA.4, K.OA.5, K.NBT.1, K.MD.3, K.G.1, K.G.2, K.G.3, K.G.4, K.G.5, K.G.6** and all Mathematical Practices.

Carta a la familia

Un vistazo general al contenido

Estimada familia:

En el programa de matemáticas de su niño, las partes son números que se juntan para formar otros números, por ejemplo:

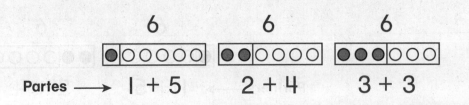

Partes ⟶ 1 + 5   2 + 4   3 + 3

Conocer las partes de los números ayudará a su niño a desarrollar la comprensión de las relaciones entre los números y le dará una base firme para el aprendizaje de la suma y la resta.

Su niño ha comenzado a usar los dibujos de "Montañas matemáticas" para mostrar las partes de los números. Los niños escucharon un cuento sobre unas bolitas que viven en la cima de la "Montaña matemática". Para divertirse, las bolitas descienden rodando por el costado de la montaña. Por ejemplo:

Bolitas de la Montaña matemática ⟶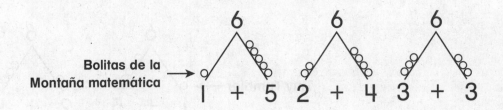

1 + 5   2 + 4   3 + 3

Se le pedirá a su niño que cuente las bolitas y que las dibuje (como se muestra arriba) para mostrar las partes. Los niños disfrutan de este apoyo visual y con la práctica continua pueden asimilar más fácilmente el concepto de partes. Si es necesario, ayude a su niño con las páginas de Montañas matemáticas.

¡Gracias!

Atentamente,
El maestro de su niño

 CA CC

En la Unidad 4 se aplican los siguientes estándares auxiliares, contenidos en los *Estándares Estatales Comunes de Matemáticas con Adiciones para California*: K.CC.1, K.CC.3, K.CC.4, K.CC.4a, K.CC.4b, K.CC.4c, K.CC.5, K.CC.6, K.CC.7, K.OA.1, K.OA.2, K.OA.3, K.OA.4, K.OA.5, K.NBT.1, K.MD.3, K.G.1, K.G.2, K.G.3, K.G.4, K.G.5, K.G.6 y todos los de prácticas matemáticas.

Name _____

CA CC Content Standards **K.CC.1, K.OA.1, K.OA2, K.OA.5**
Mathematical Practices **MP.1, MP.2, MP.4**

VOCABULARY
add

I. **Add** the numbers.

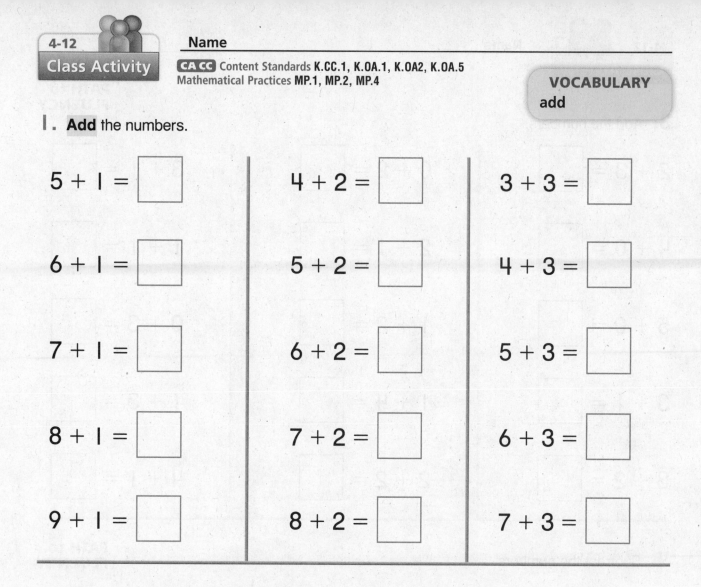

$5 + 1 = \boxed{}$ $4 + 2 = \boxed{}$ $3 + 3 = \boxed{}$

$6 + 1 = \boxed{}$ $5 + 2 = \boxed{}$ $4 + 3 = \boxed{}$

$7 + 1 = \boxed{}$ $6 + 2 = \boxed{}$ $5 + 3 = \boxed{}$

$8 + 1 = \boxed{}$ $7 + 2 = \boxed{}$ $6 + 3 = \boxed{}$

$9 + 1 = \boxed{}$ $8 + 2 = \boxed{}$ $7 + 3 = \boxed{}$

2. Connect the dots in order.

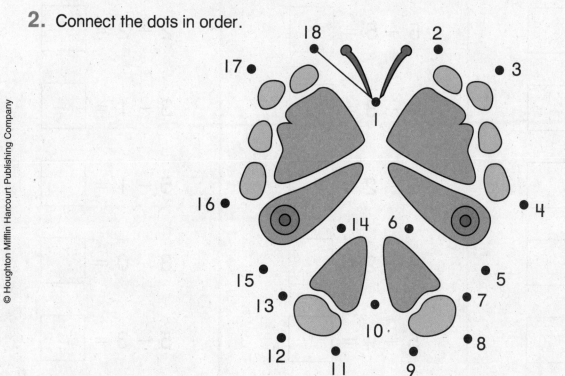

3. Add the numbers.

2 + 3 = ☐   0 + 2 = ☐   3 + 1 = ☐

4 + 0 = ☐   2 + 1 = ☐   1 + 1 = ☐

5 + 0 = ☐   1 + 2 = ☐   0 + 3 = ☐

3 + 1 = ☐   1 + 4 = ☐   1 + 3 = ☐

3 + 2 = ☐   2 + 2 = ☐   4 + 1 = ☐

4. Subtract the numbers.

3 − 2 = ☐   5 − 5 = ☐   2 − 2 = ☐

4 − 1 = ☐   4 − 3 = ☐   3 − 1 = ☐

3 − 3 = ☐   5 − 2 = ☐   5 − 1 = ☐

5 − 0 = ☐   4 − 2 = ☐   3 − 0 = ☐

2 − 1 = ☐   5 − 4 = ☐   5 − 3 = ☐

Addition Equations

CA CC Content Standards K.CC.3, K.OA.1, K.OA.3
Mathematical Practices MP.3, MP.6, MP.8

Name

1. Draw **Tiny Tumblers** on the **Math Mountains**.

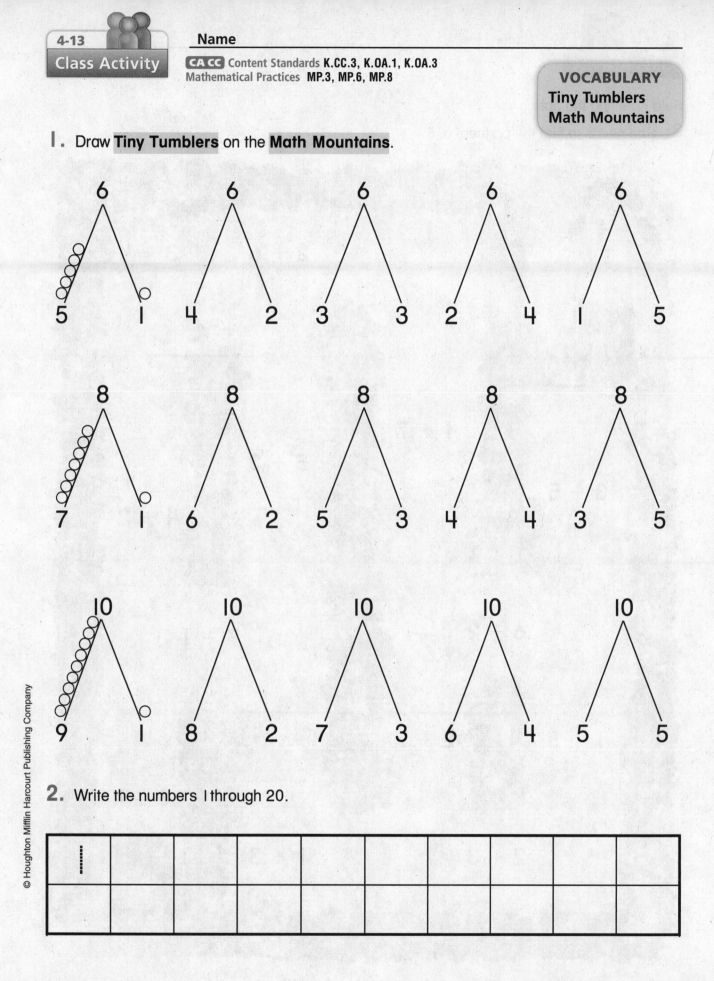

2. Write the numbers 1 through 20.

More Partners of 10 with 5-Groups **181**

Name _____

Help Kate find the gate.

3. She needs to find the partners of 8.

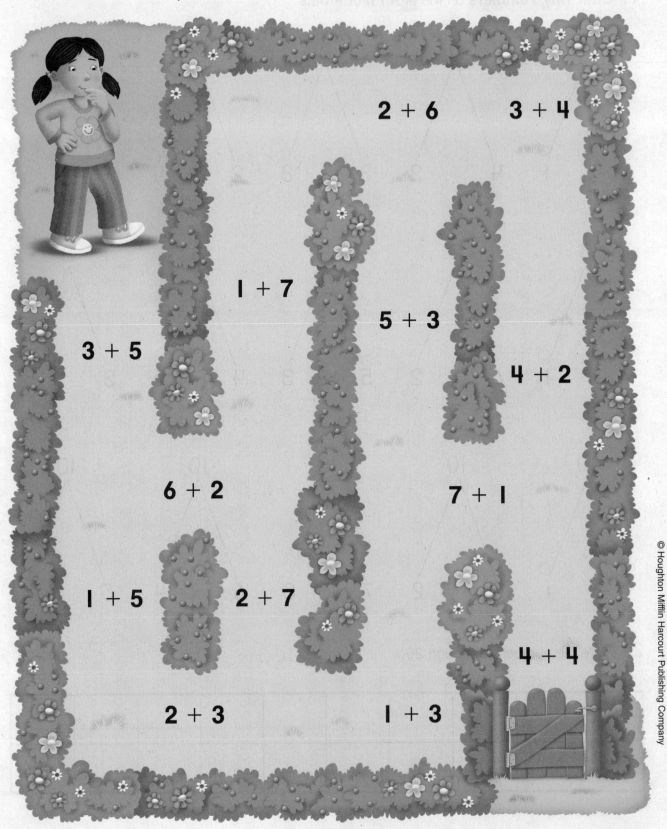

2 + 6   3 + 4

1 + 7

3 + 5   5 + 3

4 + 2

6 + 2   7 + 1

1 + 5   2 + 7

4 + 4

2 + 3   1 + 3

CA CC Content Standards **K.CC.1, K.CC.2, K.CC.4c, K.OA.1, K.OA.5** Mathematical Practices **MP.6, MP.7, MP.8**

VOCABULARY
add

1. **Add** the numbers.

$5 + 5 = \boxed{}$ $\qquad$ $6 + 2 = \boxed{}$ $\qquad$ $2 + 7 = \boxed{}$

$3 + 4 = \boxed{}$ $\qquad$ $4 + 2 = \boxed{}$ $\qquad$ $7 + 3 = \boxed{}$

$5 + 1 = \boxed{}$ $\qquad$ $4 + 4 = \boxed{}$ $\qquad$ $5 + 4 = \boxed{}$

$3 + 6 = \boxed{}$ $\qquad$ $5 + 2 = \boxed{}$ $\qquad$ $5 + 3 = \boxed{}$

$4 + 6 = \boxed{}$ $\qquad$ $3 + 3 = \boxed{}$ $\qquad$ $2 + 5 = \boxed{}$

2. Connect the dots in order.

Name _____

PATH to
FLUENCY

3. Add the numbers.

4 + 1 = ☐   0 + 3 = ☐   4 + 0 = ☐

3 + 2 = ☐   1 + 4 = ☐   1 + 1 = ☐

5 + 0 = ☐   3 + 1 = ☐   1 + 3 = ☐

2 + 2 = ☐   1 + 2 = ☐   0 + 5 = ☐

2 + 1 = ☐   3 + 0 = ☐   2 + 3 = ☐

PATH to
FLUENCY

4. Subtract the numbers.

5 − 4 = ☐   5 − 2 = ☐   5 − 1 = ☐

4 − 4 = ☐   4 − 2 = ☐   4 − 3 = ☐

3 − 1 = ☐   3 − 0 = ☐   3 − 3 = ☐

2 − 1 = ☐   2 − 2 = ☐   2 − 0 = ☐

1 − 0 = ☐   1 − 1 = ☐   5 − 3 = ☐

Addition and Subtraction Equations

Class Activity

Name _____

CA CC Content Standards **K.CC.1, K.CC.3, K.CC.4a, K.CC.5, K.OA.1, K.OA.2, K.OA.5, K.NBT.1**
Mathematical Practices **MP.2, MP.7**

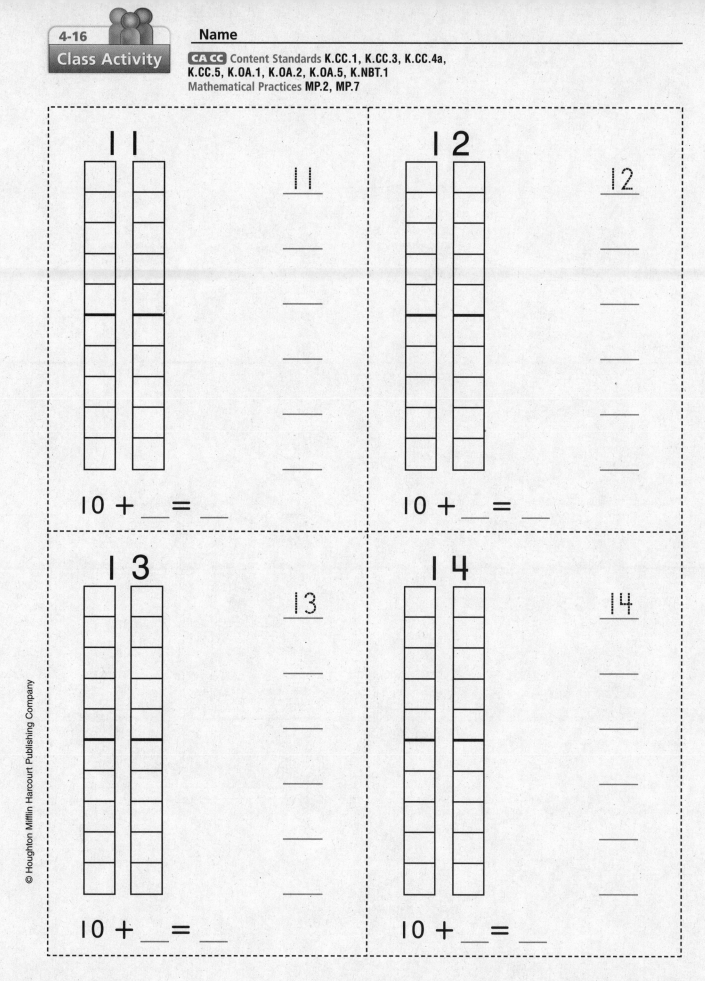

11

11

10 + __ = __

12

12

10 + __ = __

13

13

10 + __ = __

14

14

10 + __ = __

Teen Number Book **185**

1. Draw lines to match.

2. Make two matches.

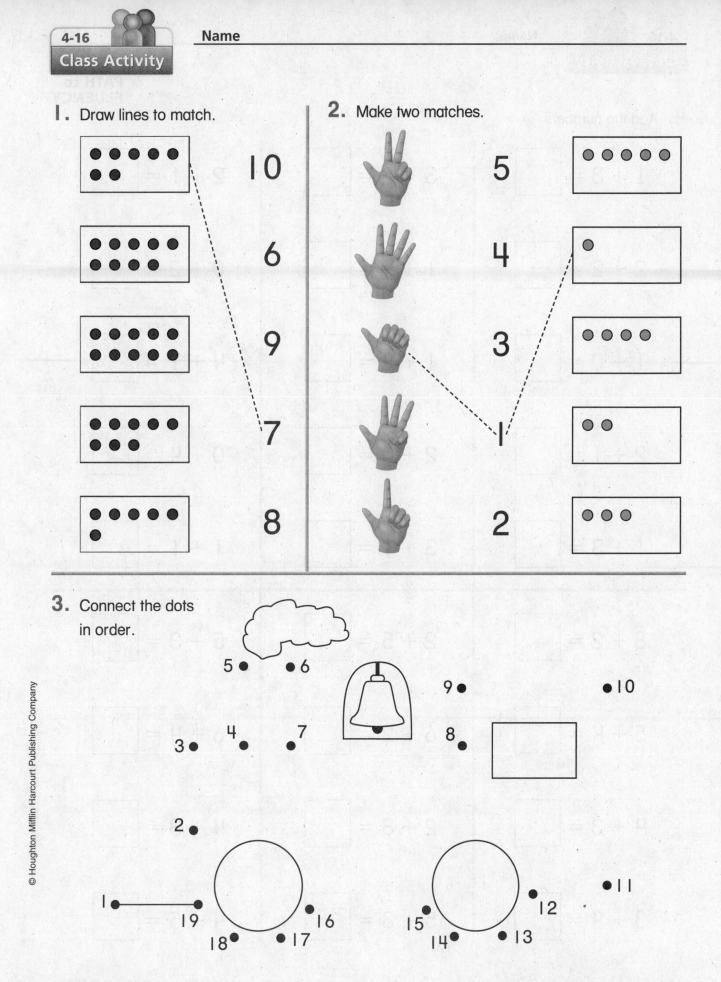

10

6

9

7

8

5

4

3

1

2

3. Connect the dots in order.

5   6

9   10

3   4   7

8

2

1   19   16

18   17   15   14   13   12   11

Name _____

4. Add the numbers.

1 + 3 = ☐   3 + 2 = ☐   2 + 1 = ☐

2 + 2 = ☐   1 + 4 = ☐   0 + 2 = ☐

1 + 0 = ☐   1 + 2 = ☐   4 + 1 = ☐

2 + 1 = ☐   2 + 0 = ☐   0 + 4 = ☐

1 + 3 = ☐   3 + 1 = ☐   1 + 1 = ☐

8 + 2 = ☐   2 + 5 = ☐   5 + 3 = ☐

5 + 4 = ☐   6 + 2 = ☐   6 + 4 = ☐

4 + 3 = ☐   2 + 8 = ☐   4 + 3 = ☐

3 + 4 = ☐   5 + 3 = ☐   4 + 5 = ☐

Teen Number Book

Name _____

CA CC Content Standards **K.CC.1, K.OA.1, K.OA.2, K.OA.5** Mathematical Practices **MP.2, MP.3, MP.6**

VOCABULARY
add

PATH to FLUENCY

1. Add the numbers.

3 + 1 = ☐

2 + 2 = ☐

0 + 4 = ☐

3 + 2 = ☐

5 + 0 = ☐

4 + 1 = ☐

2 + 0 = ☐

2 + 3 = ☐

0 + 1 = ☐

2 + 1 = ☐

3 + 0 = ☐

1 + 2 = ☐

0 + 5 = ☐

1 + 4 = ☐

1 + 3 = ☐

2. Connect the dots in order.

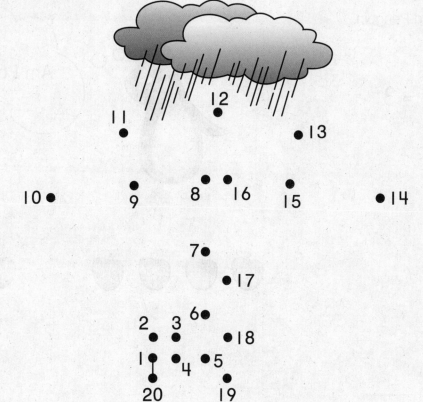

3. Subtract the numbers.

3 − 2 = ☐

4 − 1 = ☐

3 − 3 = ☐

5 − 0 = ☐

2 − 1 = ☐

5 − 5 = ☐

4 − 3 = ☐

5 − 2 = ☐

4 − 2 = ☐

5 − 4 = ☐

2 − 2 = ☐

3 − 1 = ☐

4 − 3 = ☐

3 − 0 = ☐

5 − 3 = ☐

4. Look at what Puzzled Penguin wrote.

Help Puzzled Penguin.

4 + 1 = 3

Am I correct?

4   +   1

4 + 1 = ____

Addition Equations

Name _____

CA CC Content Standards K.CC.3, K.OA.1, K.OA.2, K.OA.3, K.OA.4, K.OA.5, K.NBT.1
Mathematical Practices MP.2, MP.6

VOCABULARY
partner equation

1. Write the **partner equation.**

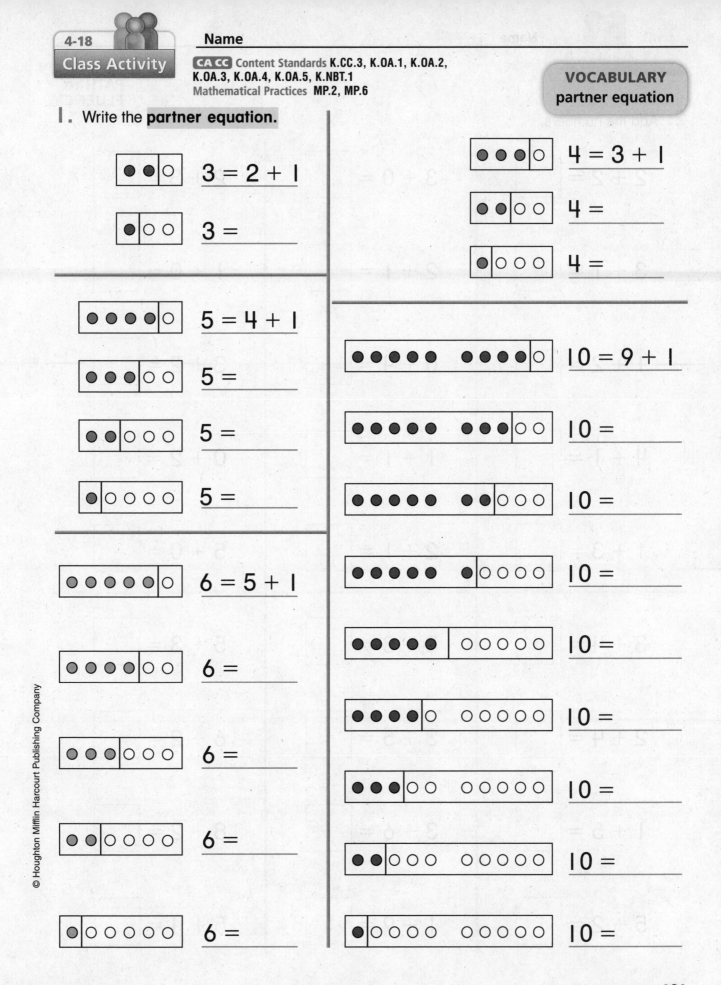

3 = 2 + 1

3 = _____

4 = 3 + 1

4 = _____

4 = _____

5 = 4 + 1

5 = _____

5 = _____

5 = _____

10 = 9 + 1

10 = _____

10 = _____

6 = 5 + 1

10 = _____

6 = _____

10 = _____

6 = _____

10 = _____

6 = _____

10 = _____

6 = _____

10 = _____

2. Add the numbers.

2 + 2 = ☐   3 + 0 = ☐   2 + 3 = ☐

3 + 1 = ☐   2 + 1 = ☐   1 + 0 = ☐

1 + 2 = ☐   0 + 4 = ☐   3 + 2 = ☐

4 + 1 = ☐   1 + 1 = ☐   0 + 2 = ☐

1 + 3 = ☐   2 + 1 = ☐   5 + 0 = ☐

3 + 4 = ☐   3 + 3 = ☐   5 + 3 = ☐

2 + 4 = ☐   3 + 5 = ☐   6 + 2 = ☐

1 + 5 = ☐   3 + 6 = ☐   8 + 2 = ☐

5 + 2 = ☐   1 + 9 = ☐   5 + 4 = ☐

Partners and Equations

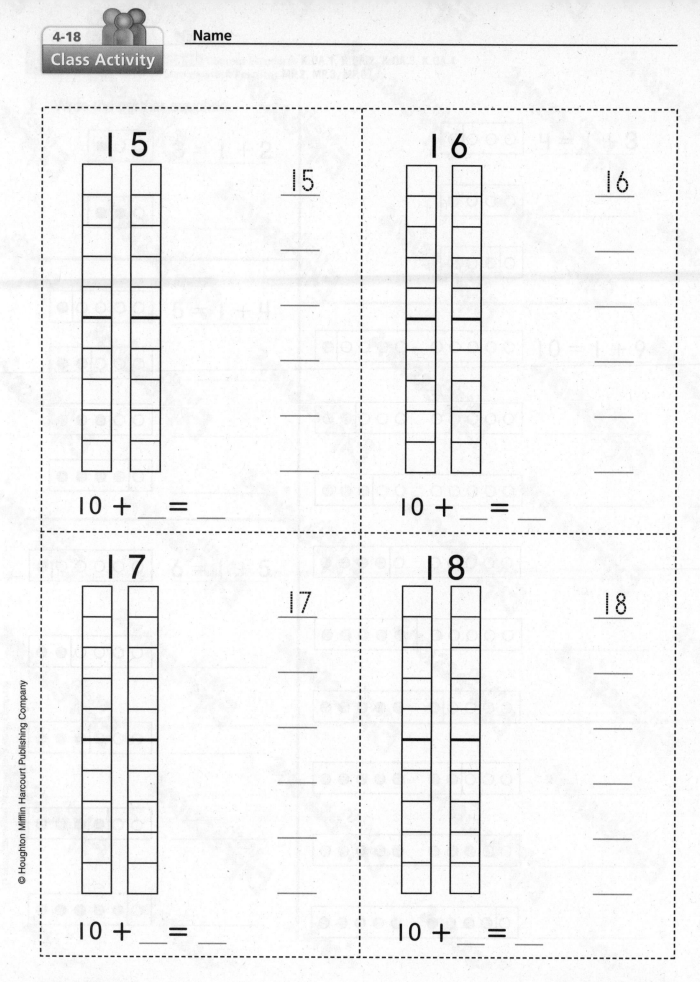

15

15
___
___
___
___
___
___

10 + __ = __

16

16
___
___
___
___
___
___

10 + __ = __

17

17
___
___
___
___
___
___

10 + __ = __

18

18
___
___
___
___
___
___

10 + __ = __

Class Activity

Name _____

2. Subtract the numbers.

9 − 1 = ☐   8 − 1 = ☐   9 − 5 = ☐

10 − 4 = ☐   9 − 2 = ☐   7 − 2 = ☐

10 − 3 = ☐   8 − 4 = ☐   6 − 1 = ☐

7 − 4 = ☐   6 − 5 = ☐   10 − 2 = ☐

6 − 3 = ☐   6 − 4 = ☐   8 − 2 = ☐

3. Look at what Puzzled Penguin wrote.

Help Puzzled Penguin.

6 = 4 - 2

Am I correct?

_____

Write Addition Equations

Name

CA CC Content Standards **K.CC.3, K.CC.4a, K.CC.4b,
K.CC.6, K.CC.7, K.OA.1, K.OA.2, K.OA.5, K.NBT.1**
Mathematical Practices **MP.4, MP.5, MP.6, MP.7**

1 9

19

10 + ___ = ___

2 0

20

10 + ___ = ___

My

Unit 4

Teen Number

Book

By _____

↖ Fold here.

1. Draw lines to match.

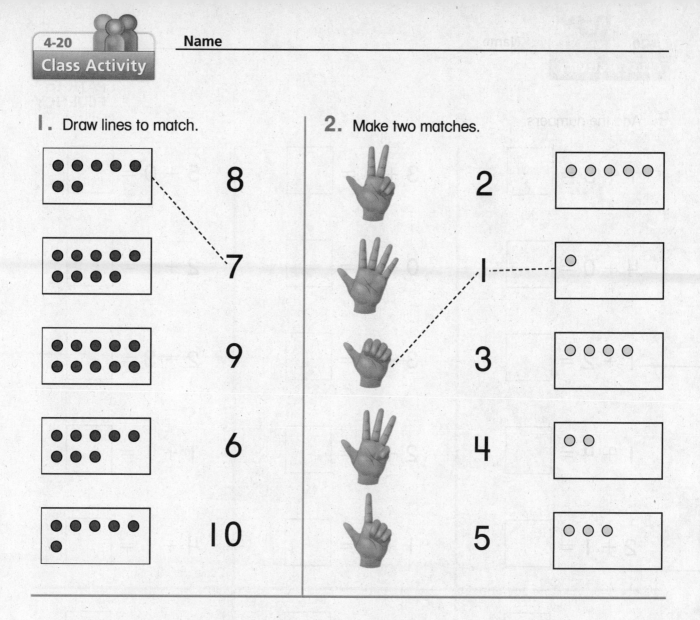

2. Make two matches.

3. Count and write the number. Ring the number that is less.

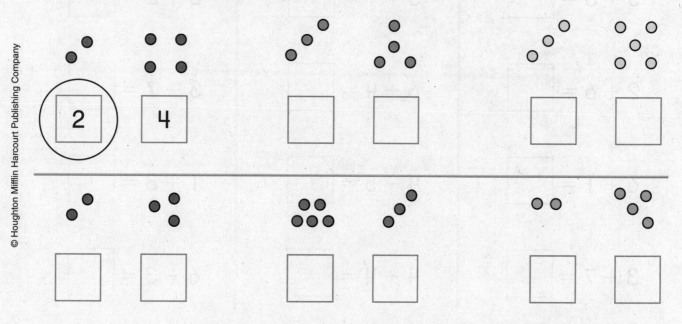

4. Add the numbers.

$1 + 3 = \boxed{}$ $3 + 1 = \boxed{}$ $5 + 0 = \boxed{}$

$4 + 0 = \boxed{}$ $0 + 2 = \boxed{}$ $2 + 1 = \boxed{}$

$1 + 2 = \boxed{}$ $3 + 2 = \boxed{}$ $2 + 3 = \boxed{}$

$1 + 4 = \boxed{}$ $2 + 2 = \boxed{}$ $1 + 1 = \boxed{}$

$2 + 1 = \boxed{}$ $1 + 2 = \boxed{}$ $4 + 1 = \boxed{}$

$5 + 3 = \boxed{}$ $5 + 1 = \boxed{}$ $8 + 2 = \boxed{}$

$2 + 6 = \boxed{}$ $6 + 4 = \boxed{}$ $3 + 7 = \boxed{}$

$6 + 1 = \boxed{}$ $4 + 5 = \boxed{}$ $1 + 8 = \boxed{}$

$3 + 7 = \boxed{}$ $4 + 4 = \boxed{}$ $6 + 3 = \boxed{}$

Name _____

CA CC Content Standards **K.G.2, K.G.4, K.G.5**
Mathematical Practices **MP.5, MP.6**

1. Look at each shape. Write the number of faces.

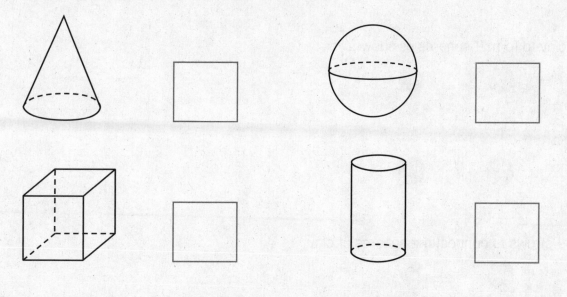

---

2. Does the shape stack or roll? Mark an X.

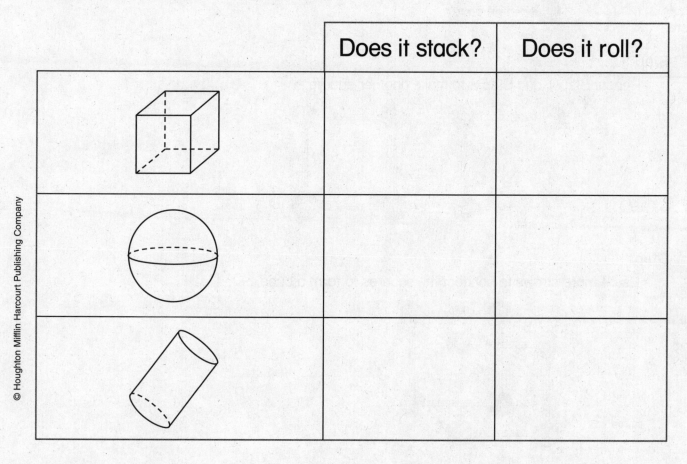

	Does it stack?	Does it roll?

Name _____

Use clay and straws to make a cube.

Step 1

Use clay to form 4 spheres as shown.

Step 2

Use 4 straws to connect the spheres of clay.

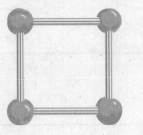

Step 3

Repeat Step 1 and Step 2 to make another square.

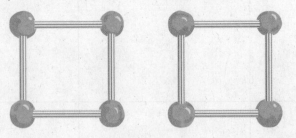

Step 4

Use 4 more straws to connect the squares to form a cube.

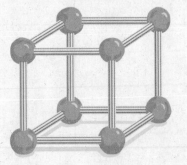

Identify Cones and Cylinders

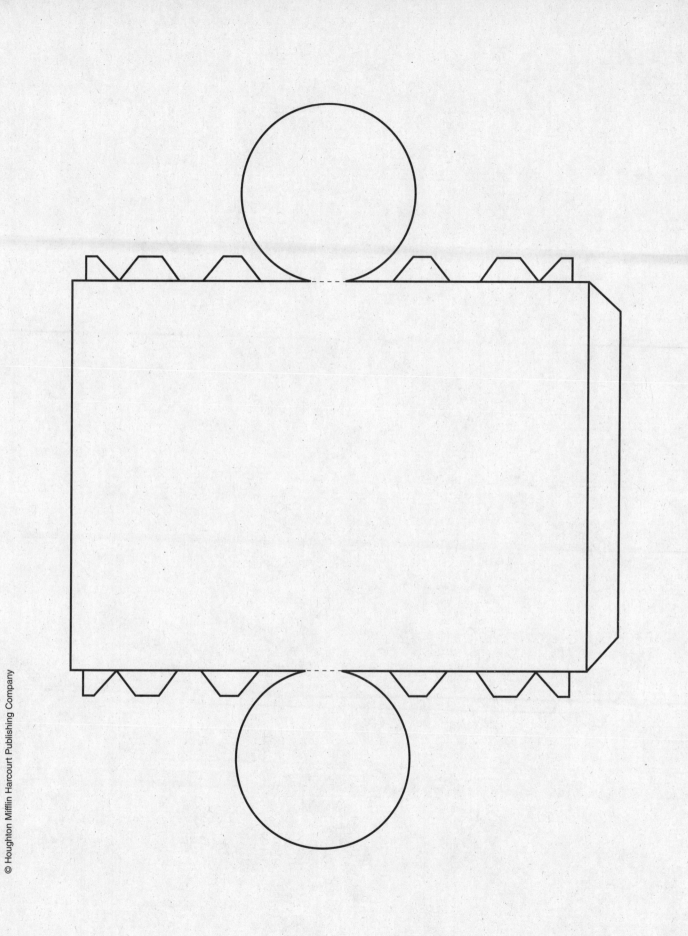

Cylinder Pattern

Name _____

CA CC Content Standards **K.G.1, K.G.2, K.G.4**
Mathematical Practices **MP.1, MP.3, MP.6, MP.7**

1. Circle the objects shaped like cubes on the top shelf. Circle the objects shaped like cylinders on the middle shelf. Circle the objects shaped like spheres on the bottom shelf.

2. Color each kind of shape.

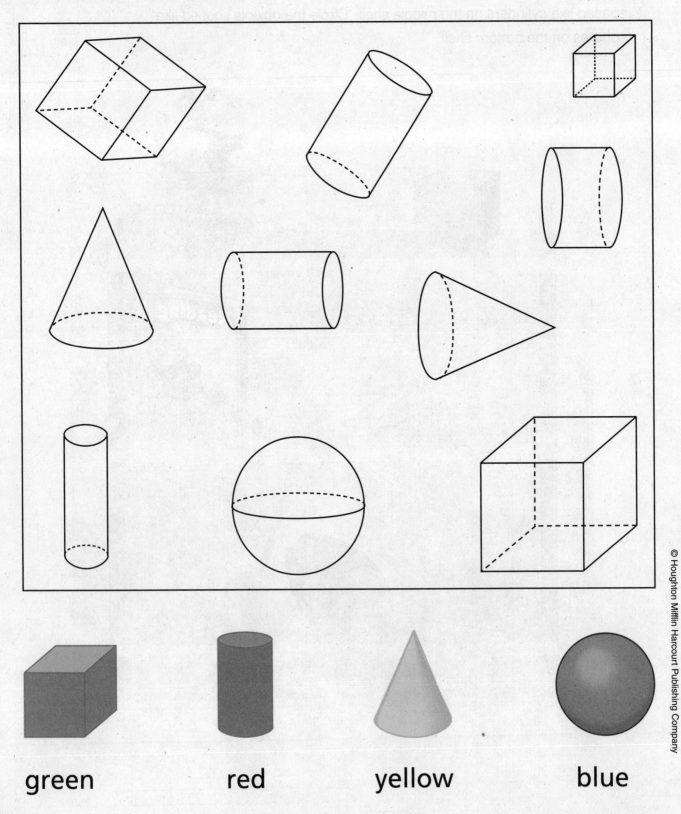

green   red   yellow   blue

1. Count to find how many apples. Write the partners.

$10 = \boxed{} + \boxed{}$

2. The store has 9 apples. Dad buys 3 apples.
Draw the apples the store has left.

3. Which partner of 10 does the picture show?

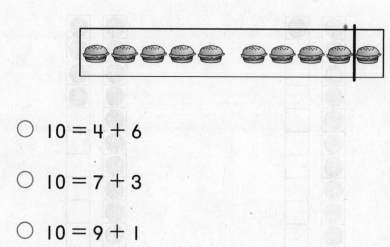

○ $10 = 4 + 6$

○ $10 = 7 + 3$

○ $10 = 9 + 1$

4. Subtract. Ring the answer.

$5 - 1 =$

4
6

5. Add. Ring the answer.

$5 + 0 =$

0
5

Count and write the number. Ring the number that is less.

6.

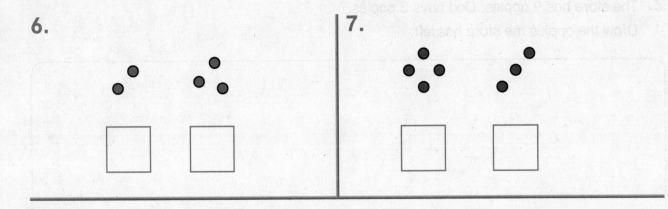

7.

8. Draw lines to match the equation to the drawing.

$10 + 4 = 14$ $10 + 3 = 13$ $10 + 1 = 11$

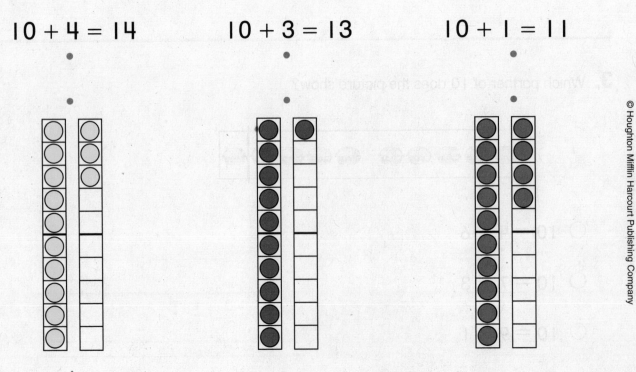

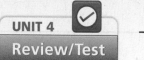
9. Choose all of the pictures that are solid shapes.

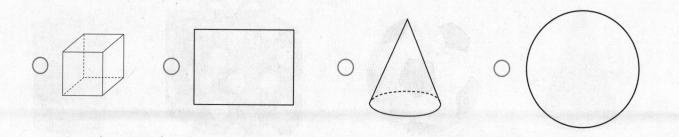

○   ○   ○   ○

Use the picture below to complete Exercises 10–13.

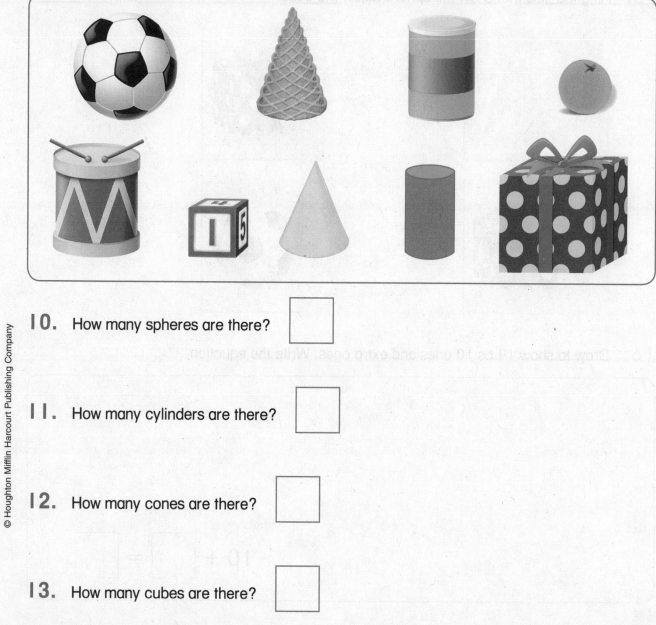

10. How many spheres are there?

11. How many cylinders are there?

12. How many cones are there?

13. How many cubes are there?

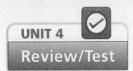
14. Ring the cylinder that is next to the cube.

15. Ring the tiles that show the sphere below the cube.

16. Draw to show 14 as 10 ones and extra ones. Write the equation.

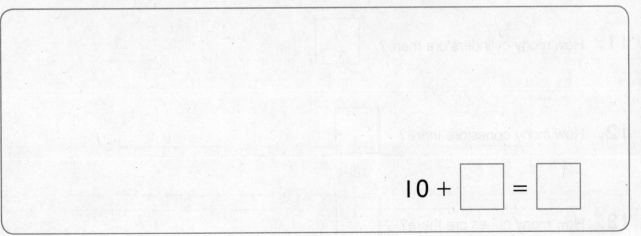

10 + ☐ = ☐

Family Letter

Content Overview

Dear Family:

We are starting a new unit in math: Consolidation of Concepts. This unit builds on the concepts that were introduced in previous units. For example, children will be creating and solving simple story problems, and making shape pictures. Math projects will include making Teen Number Books and a Night Sky display with stars in groups of ten.

Special emphasis will be on the teen numbers. Here are some ways you can help your child understand teen numbers:

- Make a game of finding teen numbers on signs and in printed materials.
- Encourage your child to count everyday objects (groups of 11–19 items). Ask your child to regroup the objects to show ten ones and extra ones.
- Continue to assist your child with math homework pages.

Thank you!

Sincerely,
Your child's teacher

CA CC

Unit 5 addresses the following standards from the *Common Core State Standards for Mathematics with California Additions*: **K.CC.1, K.CC.2, K.CC.3, K.CC.4, K.CC.4a, K.CC.4c, K.CC.5, K.CC.6, K.CC.7, K.OA.1, K.OA.2, K.OA.3, K.OA.4, K.OA.5, K.NBT.1, K.MD.1, K.MD.2,** and all Mathematical Practices

Carta a la familia

Un vistazo general al contenido

Estimada familia:

Vamos a empezar una nueva unidad de matemáticas: Reforzar conceptos. Esta unidad se basa en los conceptos que se han estudiado en las unidades anteriores. Por ejemplo, los niños formularán y resolverán problemas sencillos y harán dibujos de figuras. Los proyectos de matemáticas consistirán en hacer libros de los números de 11 a 19 y un cartel que muestra el cielo de noche con estrellas en grupos de diez.

Se pondrá especial énfasis en los números de 11 a 19. Aquí tiene algunas sugerencias para ayudar a su niño a entender estos números:

- Invente un juego para buscar números de 11 a 19 en letreros y en materiales impresos.
- Anime a su niño a contar objetos cotidianos (grupos de 11 a 19 objetos). Pídale que reagrupe los objetos para mostrar, en cada caso, un grupo de diez unidades y otro grupo con las unidades que sobren.
- Siga ayudando a su niño con la tarea de matemáticas.

¡Gracias!

Atentamente,
El maestro de su niño

© Houghton Mifflin Harcourt Publishing Company

CA CC

En la Unidad 5 se aplican los siguientes estándares auxiliares, contenidos en los *Estándares Estatales Comunes de Matemáticas con Adiciones para California*: **K.CC.1, K.CC.2, K.CC.3, K.CC.4, K.CC.4a, K.CC.4c, K.CC.5, K.CC.6, K.CC.7, K.OA.1, K.OA.2, K.OA.3, K.OA.4, K.OA.5, K.NBT.1, K.MD.1, K.MD.2** y todos los de prácticas matemáticas.

Math Stories and Scenes with Teen Numbers

Name

CA CC Content Standards **K.CC.1, K.CC.3, K.CC.4a, K.CC.5, K.OA.4** Mathematical Practices **MP.1, MP.3, MP.6**

Count the stars. Write the number.

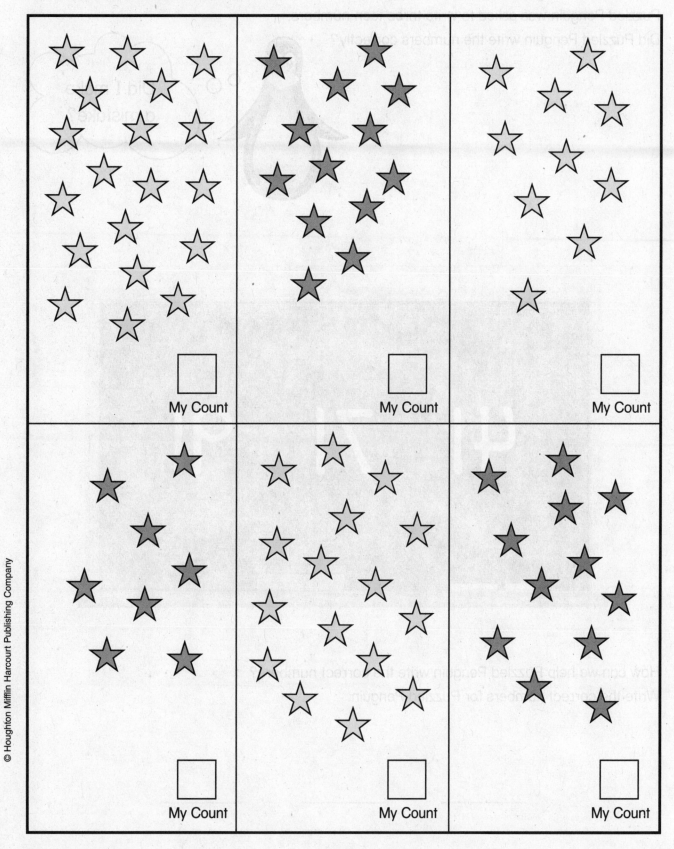

My Count

My Count

My Count

My Count

My Count

My Count

Partners of 10: Stars in the Night Sky **215**

Name _____

Help Puzzled Penguin.

Puzzled Penguin was asked to write three teen numbers.

Did Puzzled Penguin write the numbers correctly?

Did I make a mistake?

How can we help Puzzled Penguin write the correct numbers?

Write the correct numbers for Puzzled Penguin.

_____ _____ _____

Family Letter

Content Overview

Dear Family:

It is important that your child learn to see the ten in teen numbers. Each teen number (11, 12, 13, 14, 15, 16, 17, 18, and 19) is made of ten ones and some "extra ones."

Please help your child at home with groups of 11–19 objects. Ask your child to show the group of ten ones, show the extra ones, and then write the number. Below are two ways to display 17 pieces of cereal in a group of ten and extra ones, shown with a sample dialogue about the cereal.

 or

Here are some pieces of cereal. Let's find out how many pieces we have.

Can you make a 10-group?

How many extra ones do you have?

What number is a group of ten ones and 7 extra ones?

Can you write it?

If you have any questions or problems, please contact me. Thank you for your cooperation.

Sincerely,
Your child's teacher

 CA CC

Unit 5 addresses the following standards from the *Common Core State Standards for Mathematics with California Additions*: **K.CC.1, K.CC.2, K.CC.3, K.CC.4, K.CC.4a, K.CC.4c, K.CC.5, K.CC.6, K.CC.7, K.OA.1, K.OA.2, K.OA.3, K.OA.4, K.OA.5, K.NBT.1, K.MD.1, K.MD.2,** and all Mathematical Practices

Estimada familia:

Es importante que su niño aprenda a ver las decenas en los números de 11 a 19. Cada uno de estos números (11, 12, 13, 14, 15, 16, 17, 18 y 19) está formado por diez unidades más algunas "unidades adicionales".

Por favor, ayude a su niño en casa a formar grupos que tengan de 11 a 19 objetos. Pídale que muestre el grupo de diez unidades y las unidades adicionales, y que luego escriba el número. Abajo hay dos maneras de mostrar 17 rosquitas de cereal en un grupo de diez más las unidades adicionales, junto con un ejemplo de un diálogo sobre el cereal.

Aquí tenemos algunas rosquitas de cereal. Veámos cuántas rosquitas tenemos.

¿Puedes formar un grupo de 10?

¿Cuántas unidades adicionales tienes?

¿Qué número es un grupo de diez unidades más 7 unidades adicionales?

¿Puedes escribirlo?

Si tiene alguna duda o pregunta, por favor comuníquese conmigo. Gracias por su cooperación.

Atentamente,
El maestro de su niño

CA CC

En la Unidad 5 se aplican los siguientes estándares auxiliares, contenidos en los *Estándares Estatales Comunes de Matemáticas con Adiciones para California*: **K.CC.1, K.CC.2, K.CC.3, K.CC.4, K.CC.4a, K.CC.4c, K.CC.5, K.CC.6, K.CC.7, K.OA.1, K.OA.2, K.OA.3, K.OA.4, K.OA.5, K.NBT.1, K.MD.1, K.MD.2** y todos los de prácticas matemáticas.

Write the **equation**.

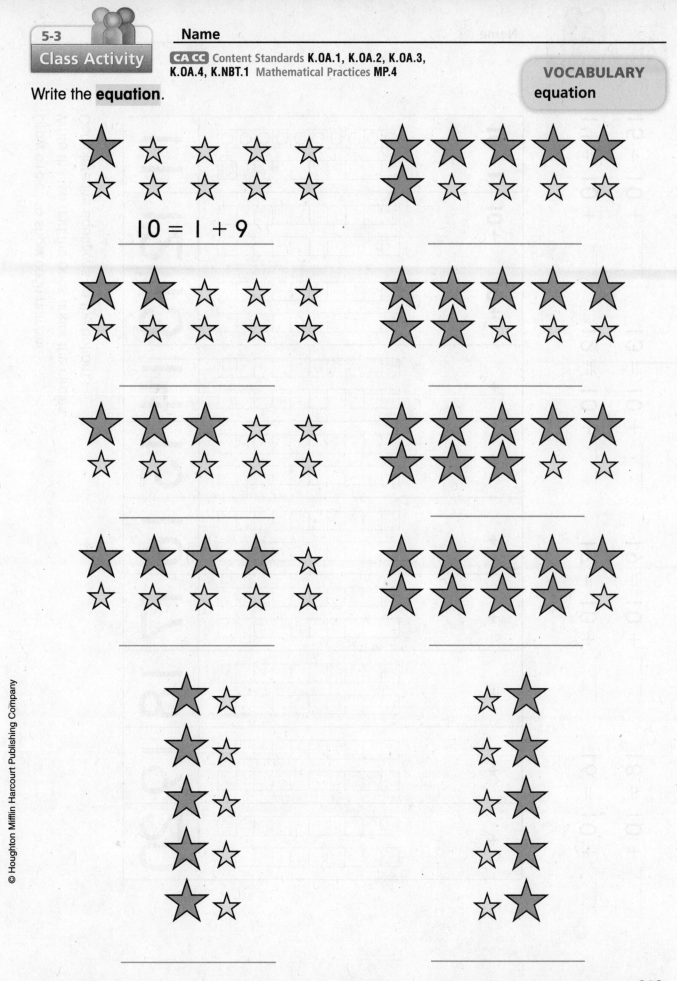

$10 = 1 + 9$

_____

_____

_____

_____

_____

_____

_____

_____

_____

Draw circles to show each number.
Write the ten and the ones under the circles.
Complete the equations on the bottom.

11	12	13	14	15	16	17	18	19	20
10+1	10+	10+	+	+	+	+	+	+	+

14 = 10 + _____

15 = 10 + _____

12 = 10 + _____

13 = 10 + _____

17 = 10 + _____

19 = 10 + _____

16 = 10 + _____

18 = 10 + _____

Name _____

CA CC Content Standards K.CC.3, K.CC.5, K.OA.1, K.NBT.1
Mathematical Practices MP.1

Ring the **ten** ones.

Write the ten ones and more **ones** in each **equation**.

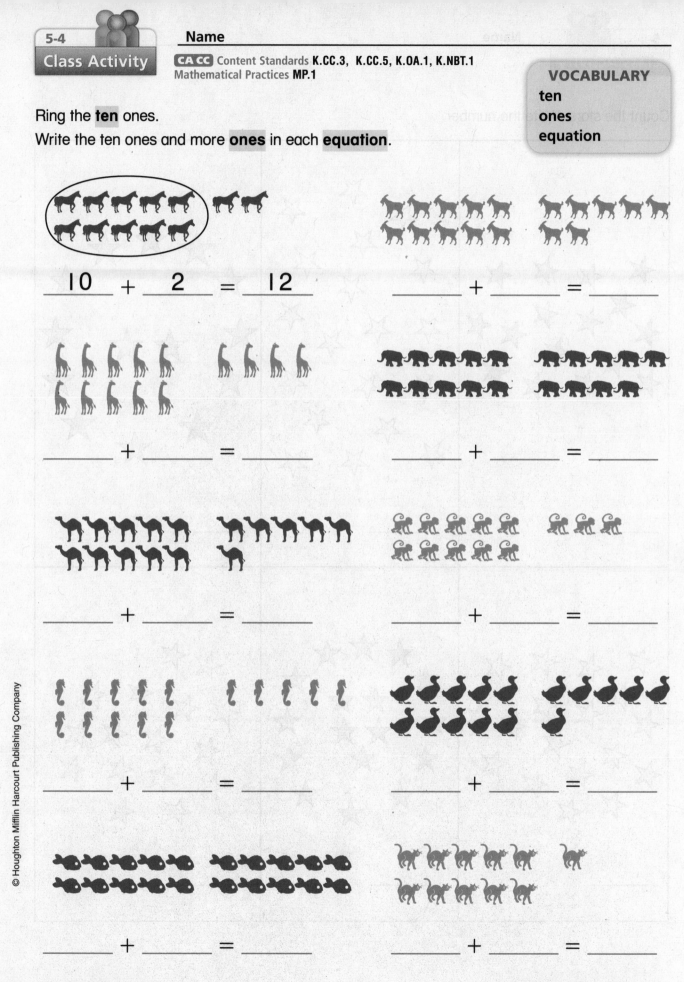

_10_ + _2_ = _12_   _____ + _____ = _____

_____ + _____ = _____   _____ + _____ = _____

_____ + _____ = _____   _____ + _____ = _____

_____ + _____ = _____   _____ + _____ = _____

_____ + _____ = _____   _____ + _____ = _____

Name

Count the stars. Write the number.

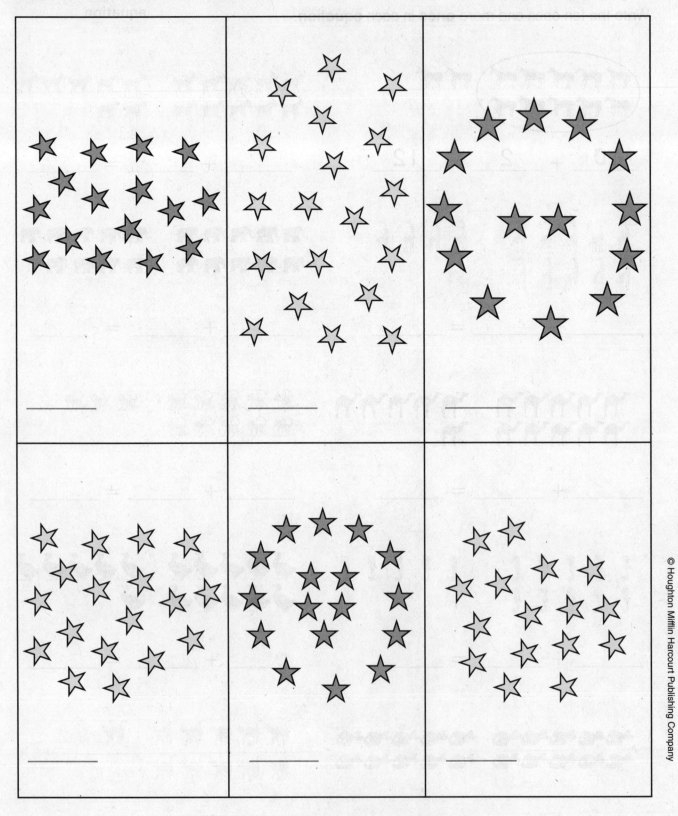

Solve and Retell Story Problems

Name _____

CA CC Content Standards **K.CC.1, K.CC.3**
Mathematical Practices **MP.4, MP.5**

Write the numbers 1–100 in vertical columns.

Ring the bottom row of numbers.

Say these numbers in order to count by tens.

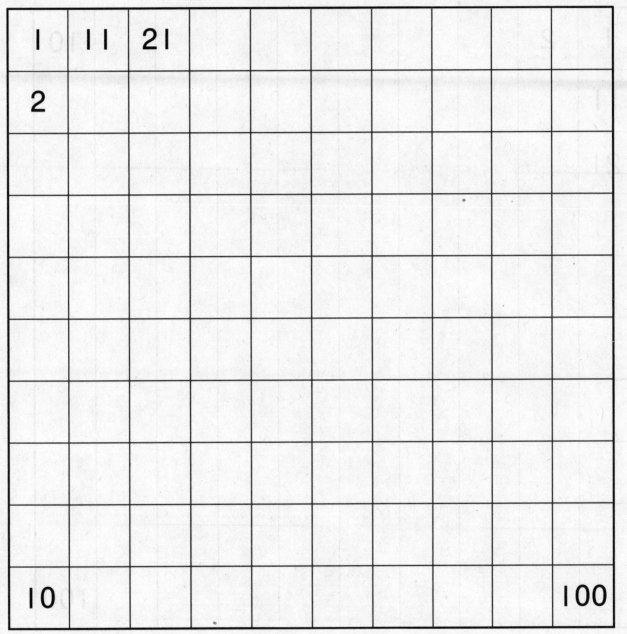

1	11	21							
2									
10									100

Make Quantities 1–20 **223**

Name _____

Write the numbers 1–100 in horizontal rows.

Ring the last column of numbers.

Say these numbers in order to count by tens.

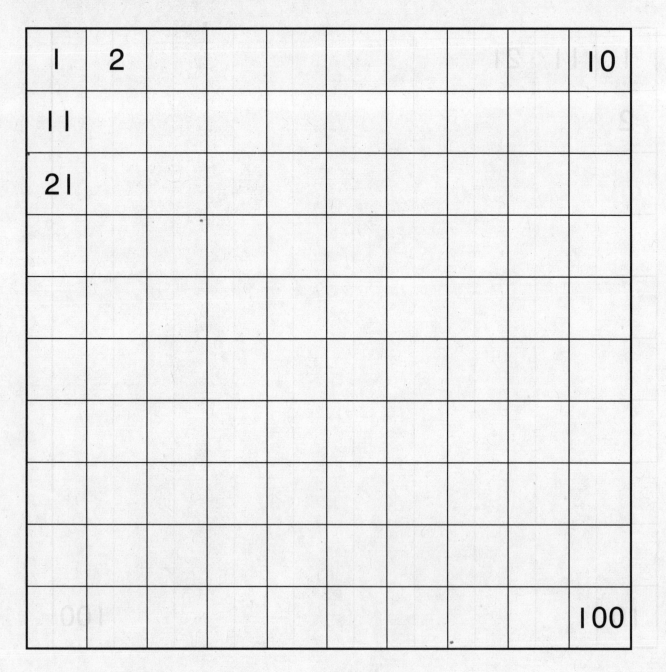

1	2								10
11									
21									
									100

Make Quantities 1–20

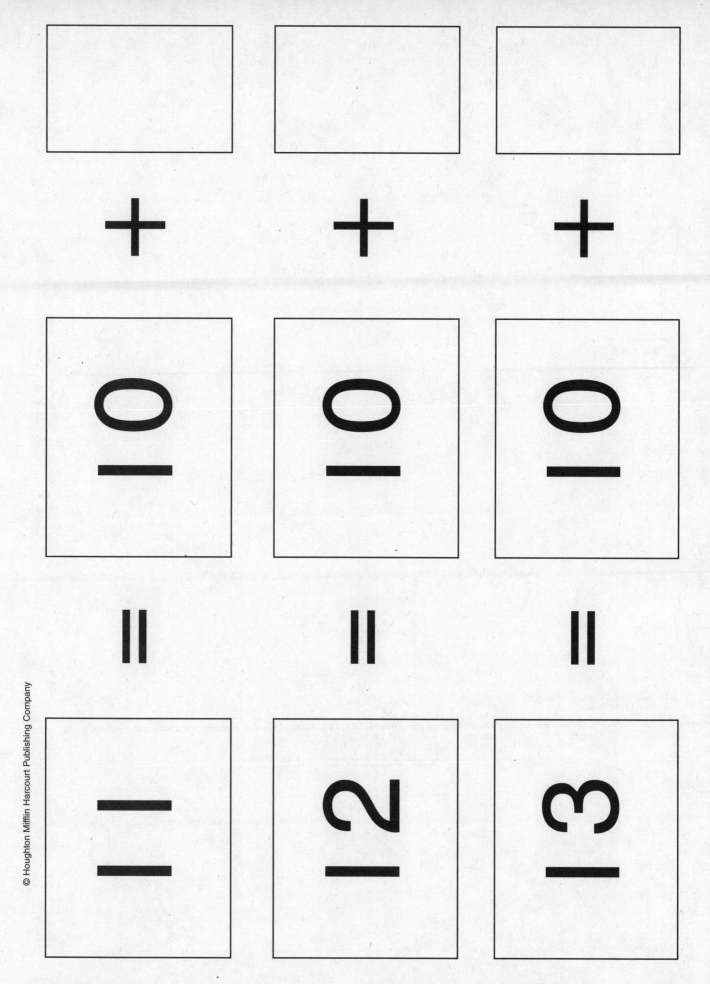

Hiding Zero Gameboard 11–13

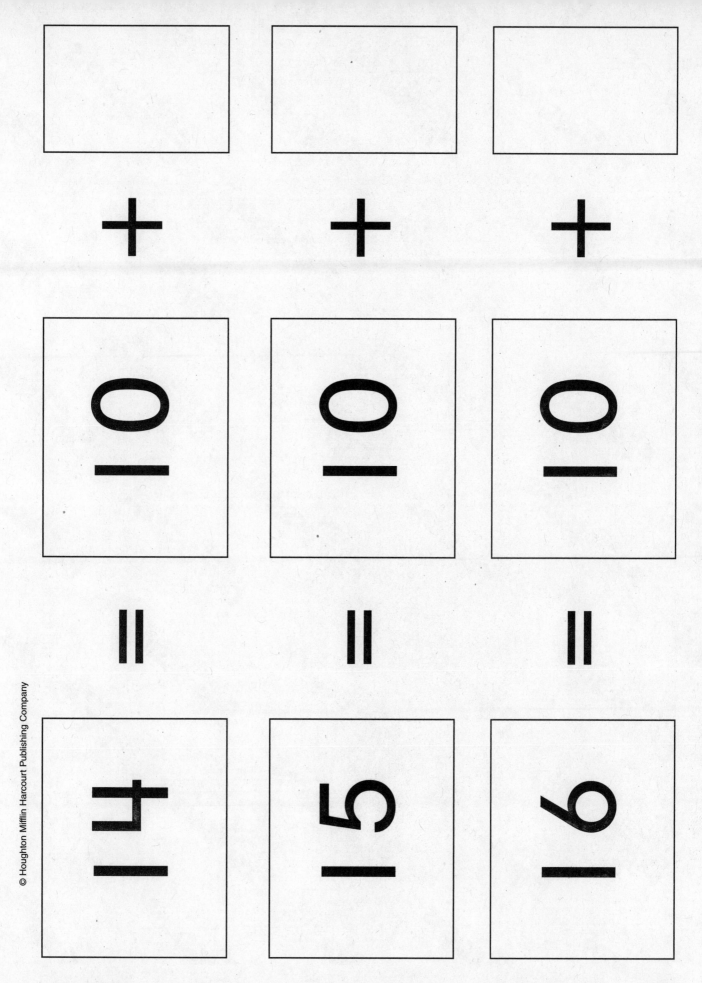

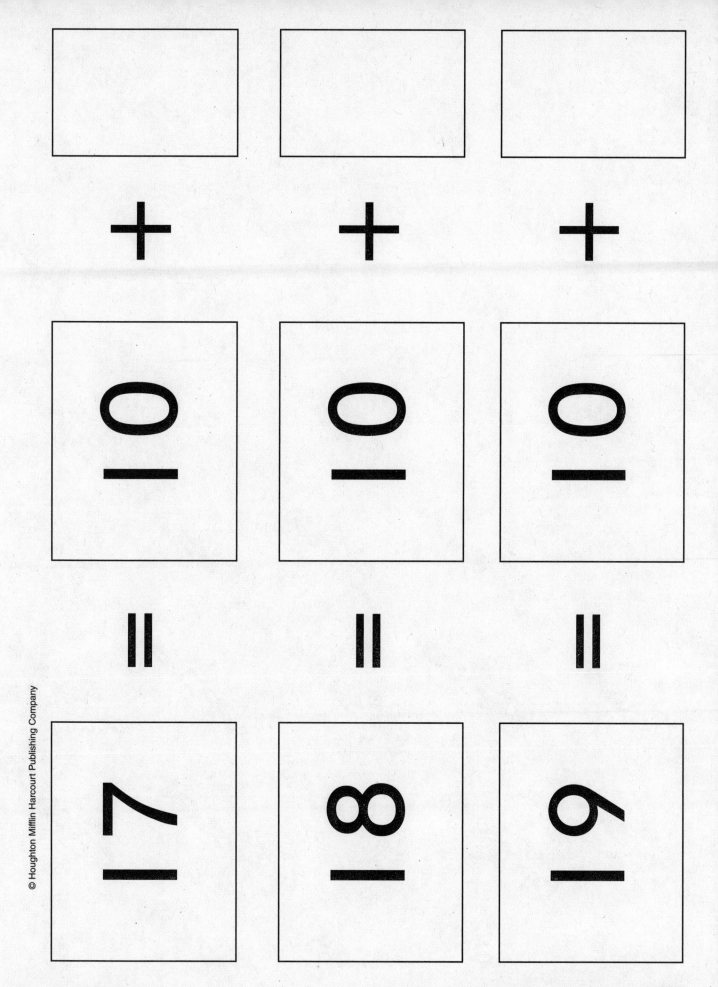

I. Write the 5- **partners**.

5

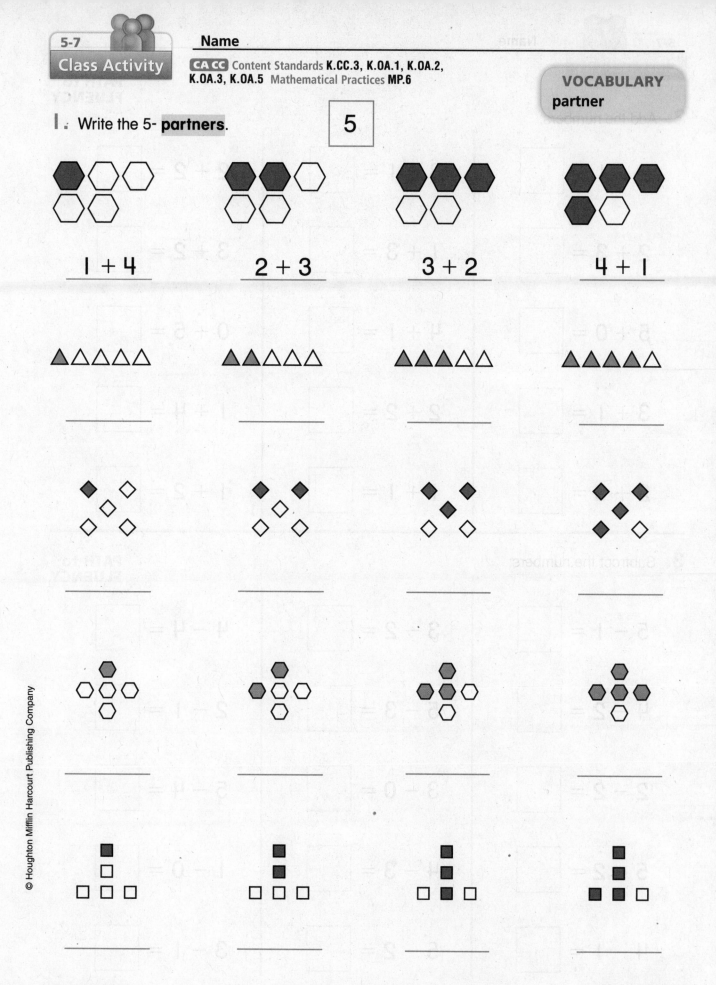

1 + 4   2 + 3   3 + 2   4 + 1

2. Add the numbers.

2 + 1 = ☐   3 + 1 = ☐   2 + 2 = ☐

2 + 3 = ☐   1 + 3 = ☐   3 + 2 = ☐

5 + 0 = ☐   4 + 1 = ☐   0 + 5 = ☐

3 + 1 = ☐   2 + 2 = ☐   1 + 4 = ☐

2 + 3 = ☐   1 + 1 = ☐   1 + 2 = ☐

3. Subtract the numbers.

5 − 1 = ☐   3 − 2 = ☐   4 − 4 = ☐

4 − 2 = ☐   5 − 3 = ☐   2 − 1 = ☐

2 − 2 = ☐   3 − 0 = ☐   5 − 4 = ☐

5 − 2 = ☐   4 − 3 = ☐   1 − 0 = ☐

4 − 1 = ☐   5 − 2 = ☐   3 − 1 = ☐

Numbers 1–20

Name

CA CC Content Standards **K.CC.1, K.CC.3, K.OA.1, K.OA.3, K.OA.4** Mathematical Practices **MP.3**

VOCABULARY
Tiny Tumbler
Math Mountain

Draw **Tiny Tumblers** on each **Math Mountain** and write the partner.

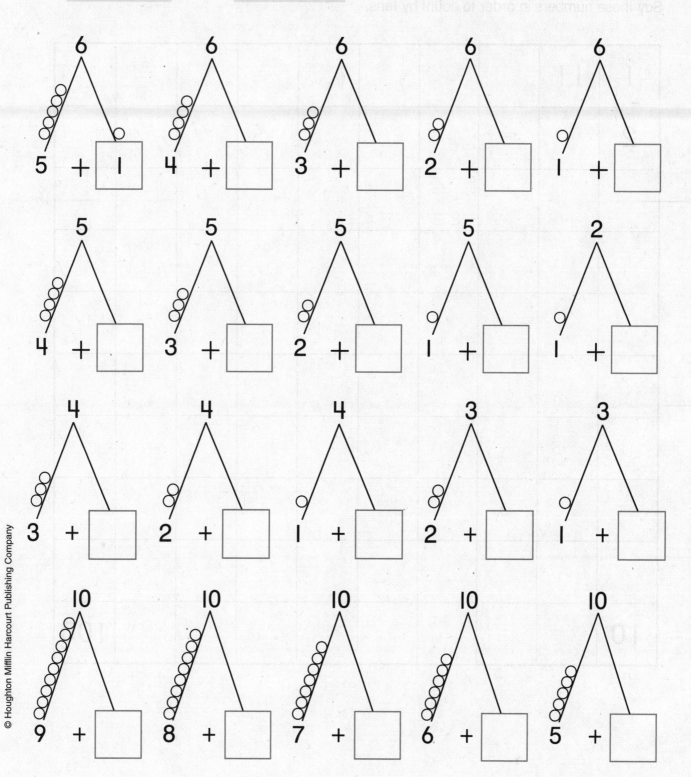

Name _____

Write the numbers 1–100.

Ring the bottom row of numbers.

Say these numbers in order to count by tens.

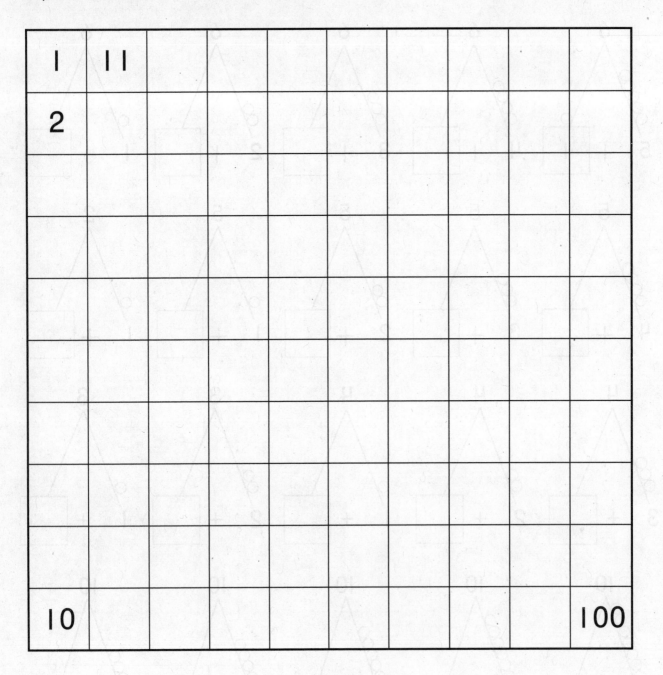

1	11								
2									
10									100

Review Partners

Name

CA CC Content Standards **K.OA.1, K.OA.3, K.OA.5**
Mathematical Practices **MP.7**

Write the 6-**partners**.

6

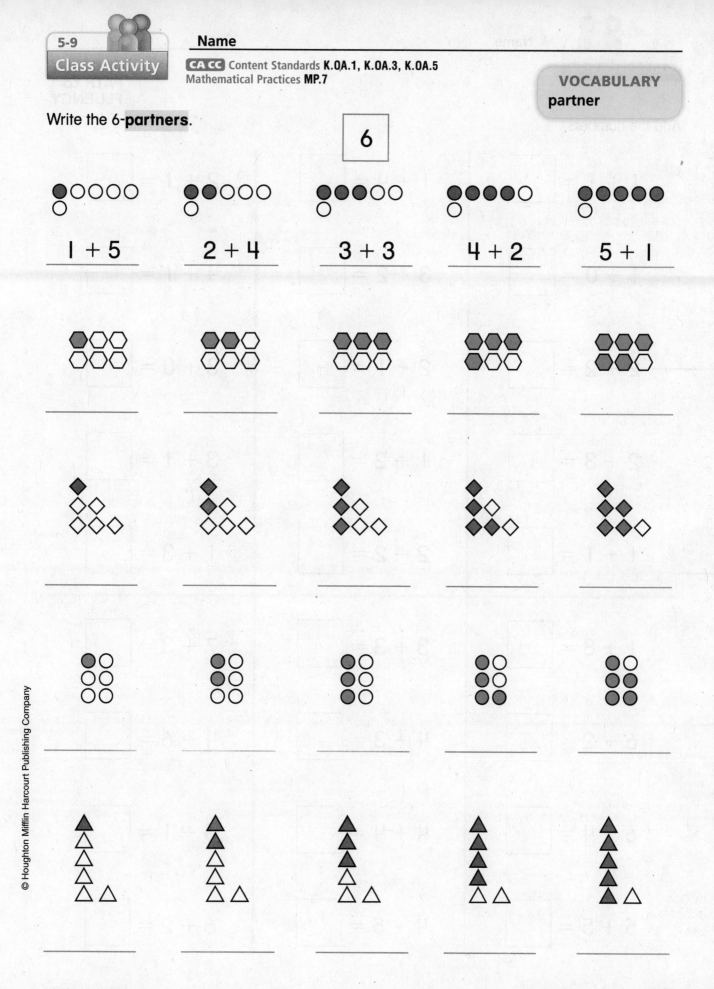

1 + 5   2 + 4   3 + 3   4 + 2   5 + 1

Name _____

Add the numbers.

$1 + 1 =$ ☐ $1 + 4 =$ ☐ $2 + 1 =$ ☐

$1 + 0 =$ ☐ $3 + 2 =$ ☐ $4 + 1 =$ ☐

$2 + 2 =$ ☐ $2 + 1 =$ ☐ $3 + 0 =$ ☐

$2 + 3 =$ ☐ $1 + 2 =$ ☐ $3 + 1 =$ ☐

$1 + 1 =$ ☐ $2 + 2 =$ ☐ $1 + 3 =$ ☐

$1 + 8 =$ ☐ $3 + 3 =$ ☐ $7 + 3 =$ ☐

$6 + 2 =$ ☐ $4 + 3 =$ ☐ $4 + 6 =$ ☐

$6 + 4 =$ ☐ $4 + 4 =$ ☐ $5 + 1 =$ ☐

$5 + 5 =$ ☐ $4 + 5 =$ ☐ $6 + 2 =$ ☐

Partners of 6, 7, 8, and 9

Name

CA CC Content Standards K.CC.2, K.CC.3, K.CC.6, K.CC.7, K.OA.1, K.OA.3, K.OA.5
Mathematical Practices MP.7

VOCABULARY
equal
unequal

PATH to FLUENCY

1. Subtract the numbers. Use your fingers or draw.

$3 - 2 =$ ☐ $5 - 5 =$ ☐ $2 - 2 =$ ☐

$4 - 1 =$ ☐ $4 - 3 =$ ☐ $3 - 1 =$ ☐

$3 - 3 =$ ☐ $5 - 2 =$ ☐ $4 - 3 =$ ☐

$5 - 0 =$ ☐ $4 - 2 =$ ☐ $3 - 0 =$ ☐

$2 - 1 =$ ☐ $5 - 4 =$ ☐ $5 - 3 =$ ☐

2. Write the symbol = or ≠ to show **equal** or **unequal**.

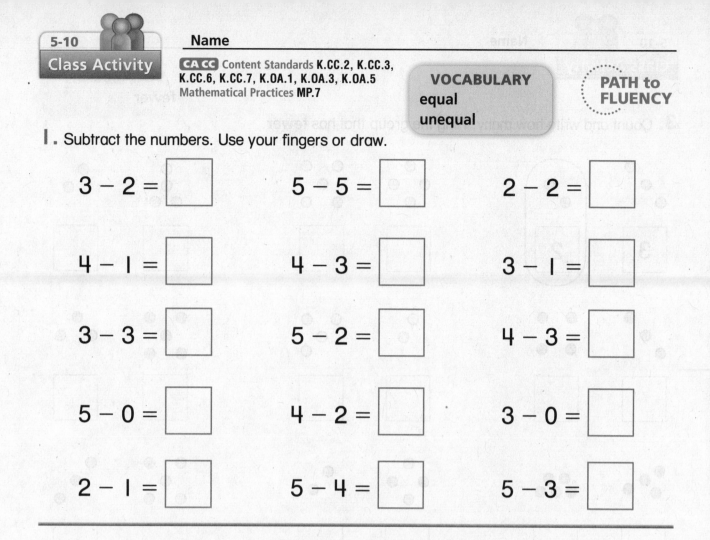

2	≠					10	2 + 8
5						6	5 + 2
3						9	3 + 4
1						7	1 + 6
4						8	4 + 4

VOCABULARY
fewer

3. Count and write how many. Ring the group that has **fewer**.

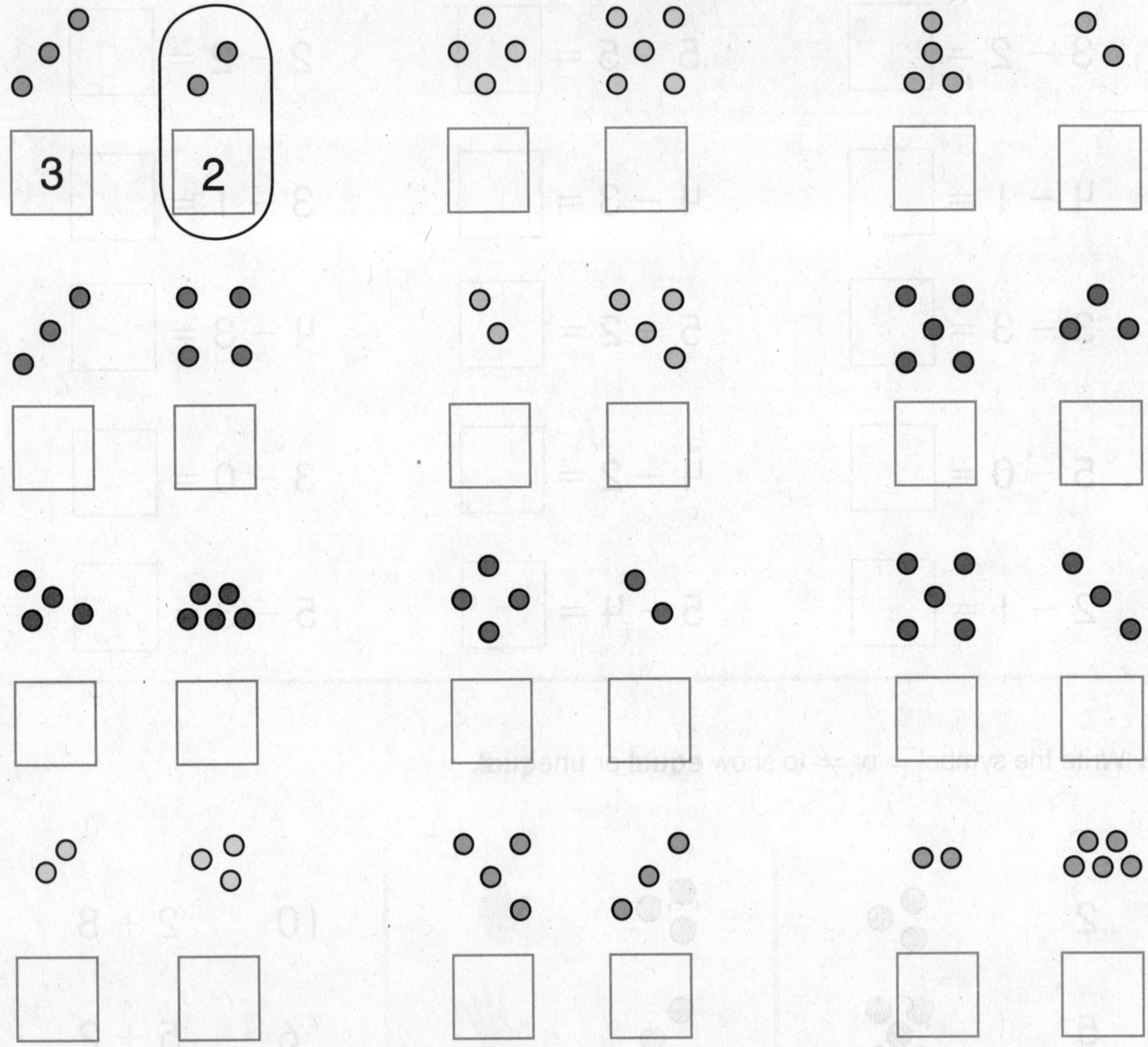

| 3 | 2 | | | | |

4. Write the numbers from 11 through 30.

11									

Tens in Teen Numbers: A Game

10

11

My
Unit 5
Teen Number
Book

By _____

For 10 and 11, draw that many things and circle 10.

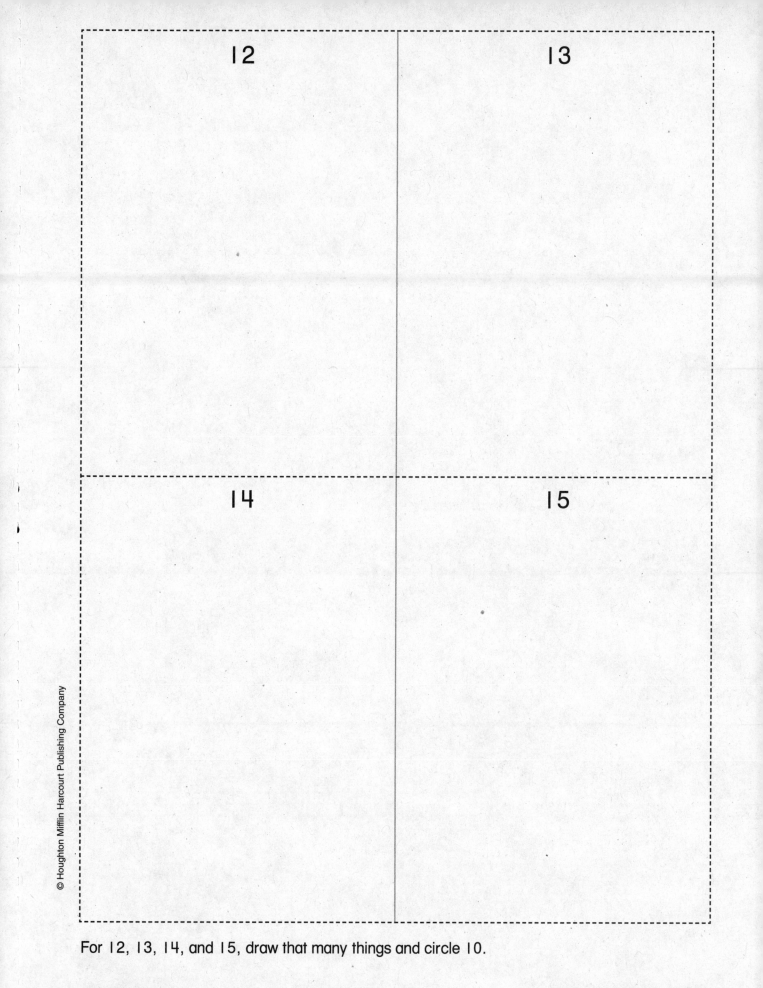

| 12 | 13 |
| 14 | 15 |

For 12, 13, 14, and 15, draw that many things and circle 10.

Tens in Teen Numbers Book **241**

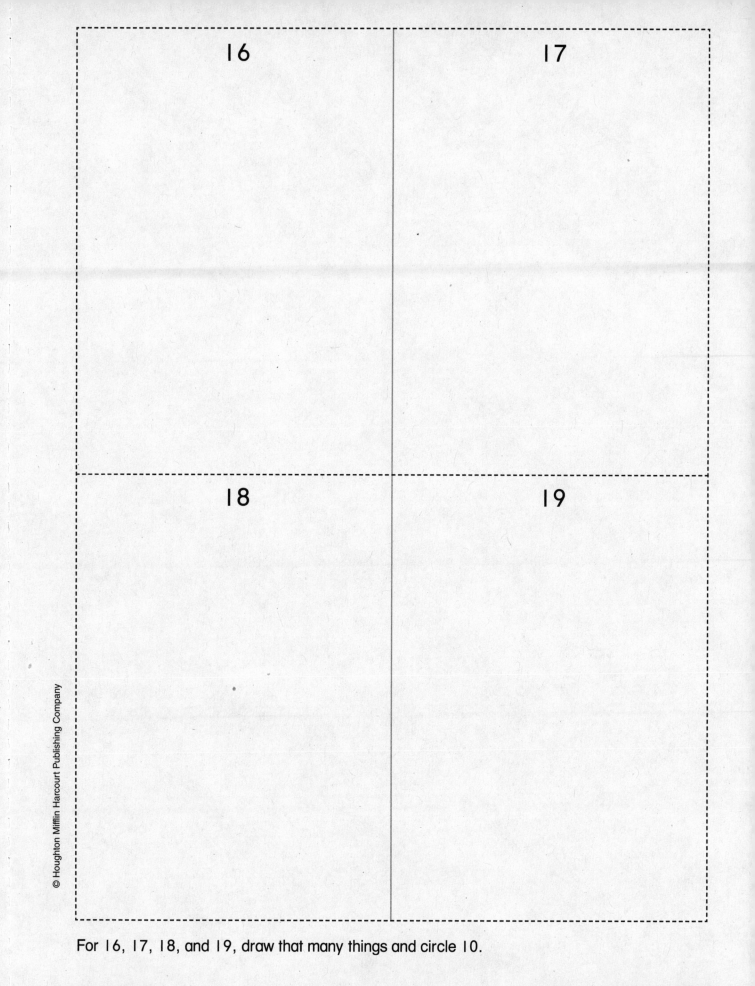

16

17

18

19

For 16, 17, 18, and 19, draw that many things and circle 10.

$$10 =$$

Partners of 10: Class Project

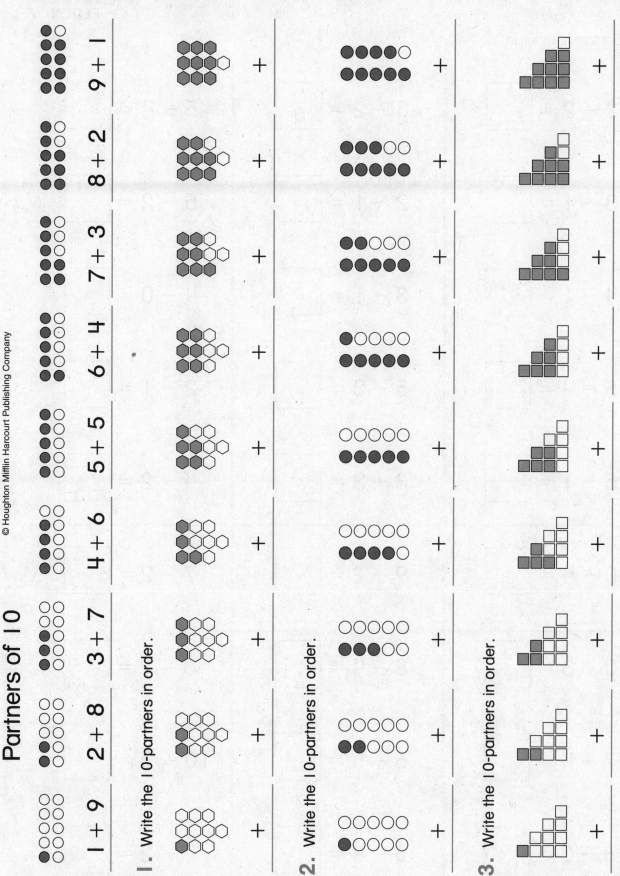

Partners of 10

9 + 1

8 + 2

7 + 3

6 + 4

5 + 5

4 + 6

3 + 7

2 + 8

1 + 9

1. Write the 10-partners in order.

2. Write the 10-partners in order.

3. Write the 10-partners in order.

Name _____

Subtract the numbers.

2 − 2 = ☐   3 − 2 = ☐   5 − 4 = ☐

3 − 1 = ☐   2 − 1 = ☐   5 − 2 = ☐

4 − 1 = ☐   3 − 1 = ☐   4 − 0 = ☐

5 − 4 = ☐   5 − 3 = ☐   2 − 1 = ☐

5 − 1 = ☐   3 − 3 = ☐   4 − 2 = ☐

10 − 4 = ☐   9 − 2 = ☐   7 − 2 = ☐

10 − 3 = ☐   8 − 4 = ☐   6 − 1 = ☐

7 − 4 = ☐   6 − 5 = ☐   10 − 2 = ☐

6 − 3 = ☐   6 − 4 = ☐   8 − 2 = ☐

Partners of 10: Class Project

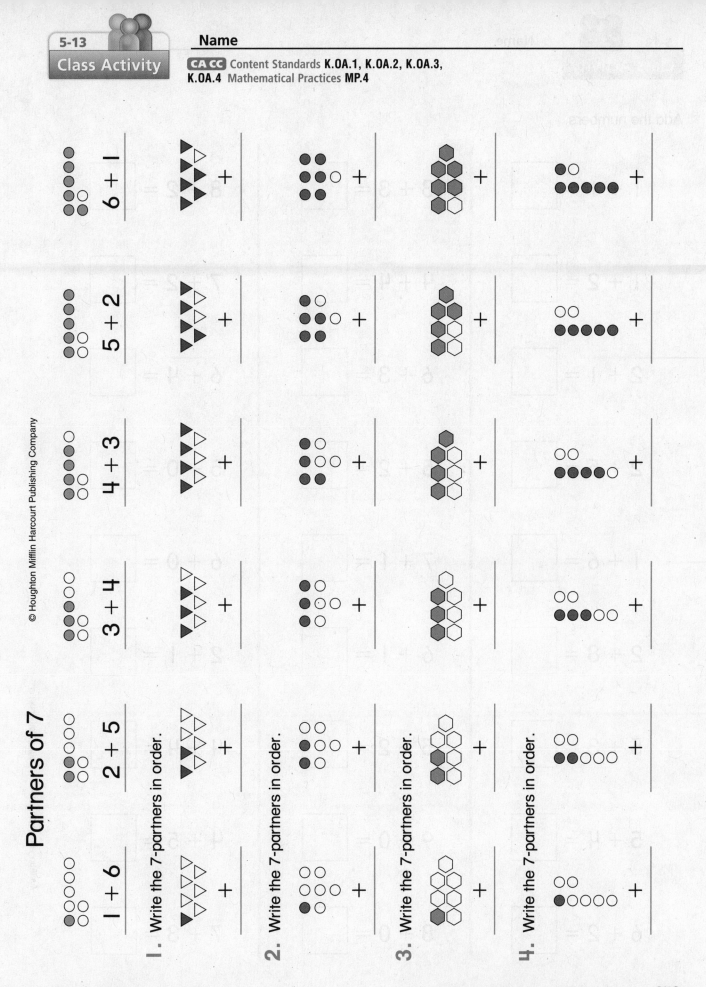

Partners of 7

6 + 1

5 + 2

4 + 3

3 + 4

2 + 5

1 + 6

1. Write the 7-partners in order.

2. Write the 7-partners in order.

3. Write the 7-partners in order.

4. Write the 7-partners in order.

© Houghton Mifflin Harcourt Publishing Company

Add the numbers.

1 + 1 = ☐   3 + 3 = ☐   8 + 2 = ☐

1 + 2 = ☐   4 + 4 = ☐   7 + 2 = ☐

2 + 1 = ☐   6 + 3 = ☐   6 + 4 = ☐

2 + 5 = ☐   5 + 2 = ☐   5 + 0 = ☐

1 + 6 = ☐   7 + 1 = ☐   6 + 0 = ☐

2 + 8 = ☐   6 + 1 = ☐   2 + 1 = ☐

5 + 3 = ☐   5 + 2 = ☐   4 + 4 = ☐

5 + 4 = ☐   9 + 0 = ☐   4 + 5 = ☐

6 + 2 = ☐   8 + 0 = ☐   7 + 3 = ☐

Match. Add shapes to make the two groups **equal**.

Write the number and the partners.

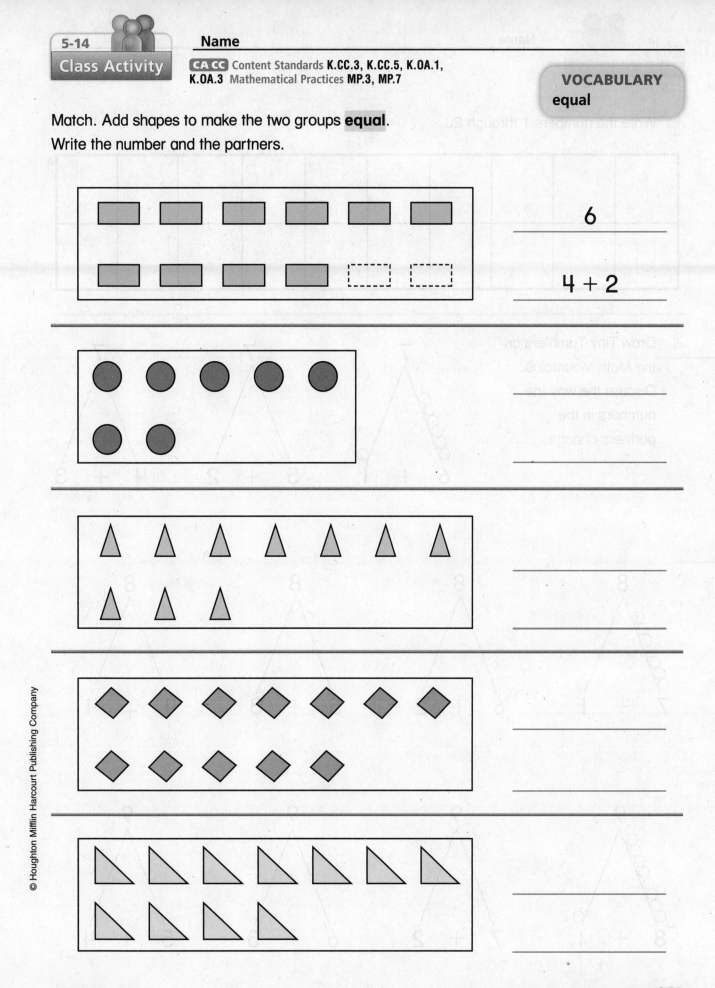

6

4 + 2

1. Write the numbers 1 through 20.

1								
11								

2. Draw Tiny Tumblers on
the Math Mountains.
Discuss the way the
numbers in the
partners change.

7
6 + 1

7
5 + 2

7
4 + 3

8
7 + 1

8
6 + 2

8
5 + 3

8
4 + 4

9
8 + 1

9
7 + 2

9
6 + 3

9
5 + 4

Name _____

CA CC Content Standards **K.OA.1, K.OA.3, K.OA.5**
Mathematical Practices **MP.2, MP.6, MP.8**

Draw Tiny Tumblers. Write how many there are on each Math Mountain.

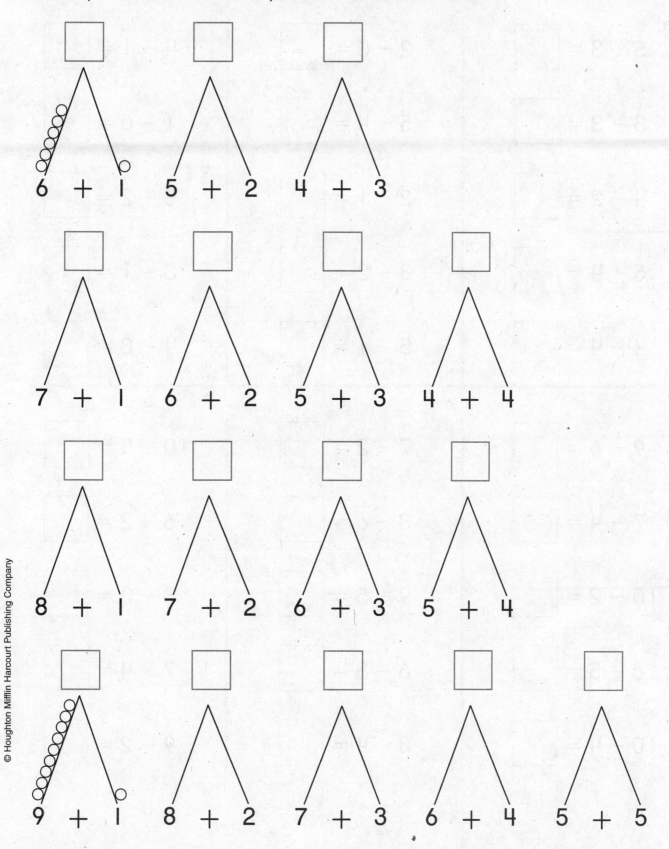

6 + 1   5 + 2   4 + 3

7 + 1   6 + 2   5 + 3   4 + 4

8 + 1   7 + 2   6 + 3   5 + 4

9 + 1   8 + 2   7 + 3   6 + 4   5 + 5

Subtract the numbers.

$5 - 3 = \boxed{}$ $2 - 0 = \boxed{}$ $4 - 1 = \boxed{}$

$3 - 3 = \boxed{}$ $5 - 4 = \boxed{}$ $1 - 0 = \boxed{}$

$4 - 2 = \boxed{}$ $2 - 1 = \boxed{}$ $5 - 2 = \boxed{}$

$5 - 4 = \boxed{}$ $3 - 2 = \boxed{}$ $3 - 1 = \boxed{}$

$4 - 4 = \boxed{}$ $5 - 1 = \boxed{}$ $4 - 3 = \boxed{}$

$9 - 6 = \boxed{}$ $7 - 2 = \boxed{}$ $10 - 5 = \boxed{}$

$7 - 4 = \boxed{}$ $8 - 6 = \boxed{}$ $6 - 2 = \boxed{}$

$10 - 2 = \boxed{}$ $9 - 5 = \boxed{}$ $8 - 3 = \boxed{}$

$8 - 5 = \boxed{}$ $6 - 3 = \boxed{}$ $7 - 4 = \boxed{}$

$10 - 4 = \boxed{}$ $8 - 4 = \boxed{}$ $9 - 2 = \boxed{}$

Add Partners to Find Totals

Name _____

CA CC Content Standards **K.CC.3, K.CC.5, K.CC.6, K.CC.7**
Mathematical Practices **MP.3, MP.6, MP.8**

Write the numbers and compare them.

Write G for **Greater** and L for **Less**.

Cross out from the greater number to make the groups **equal**.

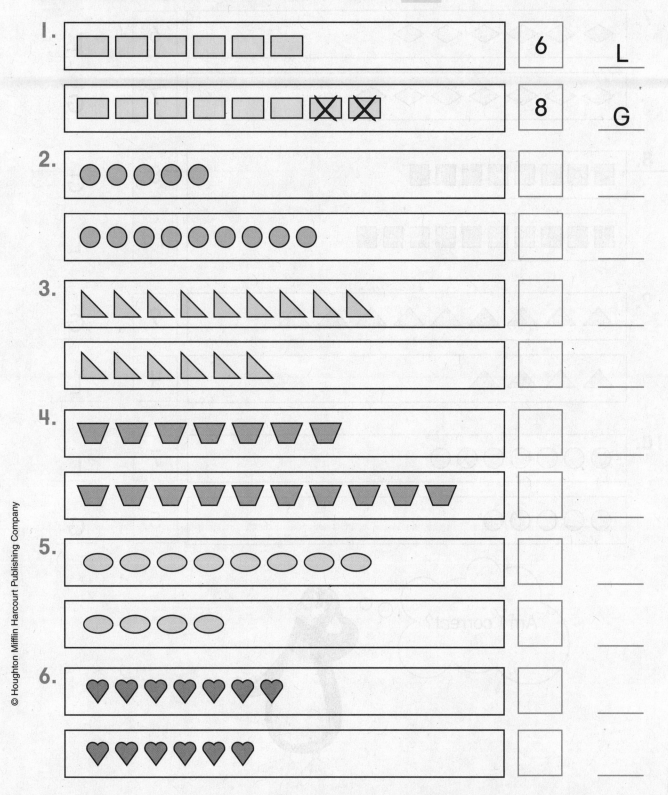

1. 6   L

     8   G

Puzzled Penguin compared groups,
writing G for Greater and L for Less.
Check Puzzled Penguin's answers.

7.

6   L

7   G

8.

8   G

10   L

9.

9   G

4   L

10.

7   L

5   G

Am I correct?

Name

CA CC Content Standards **K.CC.3, K.CC.5, K.CC.6, K.CC.7**
Mathematical Practices **MP.2, MP.3, MP.6, MP.8**

Write the numbers and compare them. Write G for **Greater** and
L for **Less**. Add (draw more) to make the groups **equal**.

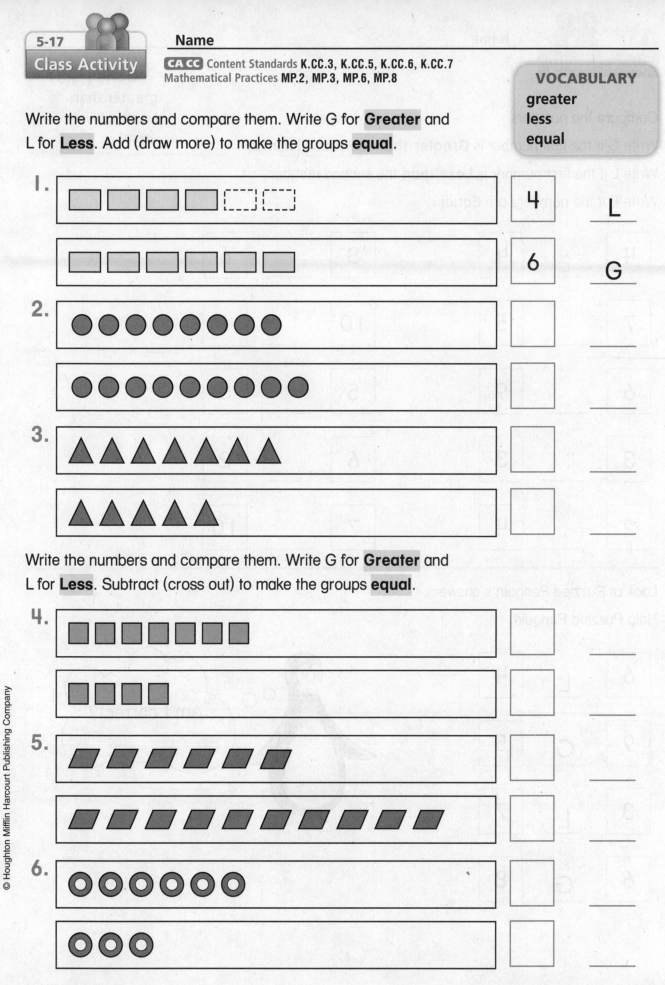

1. `4` L

    `6` G

2.

3.

Write the numbers and compare them. Write G for **Greater** and
L for **Less**. Subtract (cross out) to make the groups **equal**.

4.

5.

6.

Name _____

VOCABULARY
greater than
less than
equal

Compare the numbers.

Write G if the first number is **Greater than** the second number.

Write L if the first number is **Less than** the second number.

Write E if the numbers are **Equal**.

4	_E_	4		8	___	6
7	___	5		10	___	1
6	___	9		5	___	5
3	___	3		6	___	2
2	___	4		7	___	10

Look at Puzzled Penguin's answers.

Help Puzzled Penguin.

6	_L_	4
9	_G_	5
3	_L_	7
6	_G_	8

Am I correct?

Subtract to Make Equal Groups

Name

CA CC Content Standards **K.OA.1, K.OA.2, K.OA.3, K.OA.4, K.OA.5, K.NBT.1** Mathematical Practices **MP.2, MP.7, MP.8**

Write how many more than ten.

Draw circles to show each **teen number**.

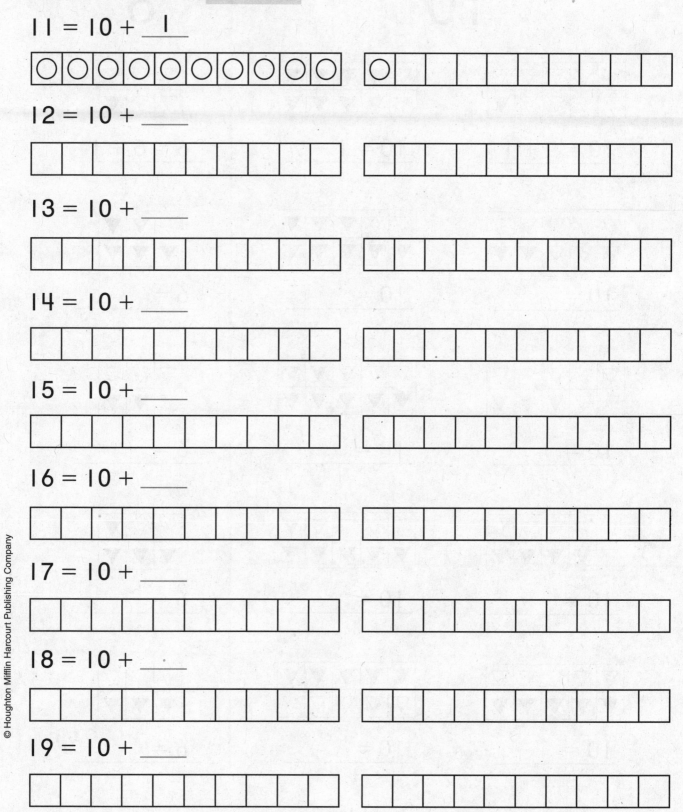

$11 = 10 + \underline{1}$

$12 = 10 + \underline{}$

$13 = 10 + \underline{}$

$14 = 10 + \underline{}$

$15 = 10 + \underline{}$

$16 = 10 + \underline{}$

$17 = 10 + \underline{}$

$18 = 10 + \underline{}$

$19 = 10 + \underline{}$

Name _____

Write the partners.

10

| 6

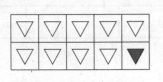

10 = 9 + 1

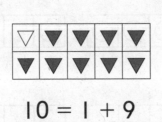

10 = 1 + 9

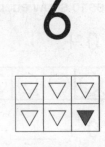

6 = 5 + 1

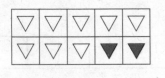

10 = _____

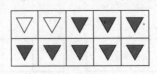

10 = _____

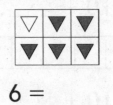

6 = _____

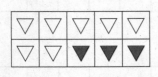

10 = _____

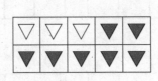

10 = _____

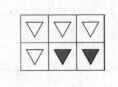

6 = _____

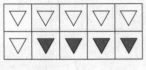

10 = _____

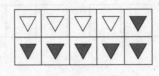

10 = _____

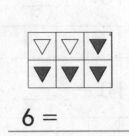

6 = _____

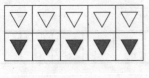

10 = _____

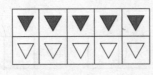

10 = _____

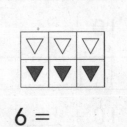

6 = _____

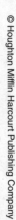

Subtract the numbers.

5 − 3 = ☐   4 − 4 = ☐   4 − 2 = ☐

5 − 4 = ☐   5 − 2 = ☐   5 − 1 = ☐

3 − 1 = ☐   3 − 2 = ☐   4 − 0 = ☐

4 − 3 = ☐   2 − 1 = ☐   5 − 5 = ☐

2 − 2 = ☐   4 − 1 = ☐   2 − 0 = ☐

9 − 1 = ☐   8 − 1 = ☐   9 − 5 = ☐

7 − 2 = ☐   10 − 5 = ☐   6 − 1 = ☐

10 − 1 = ☐   9 − 4 = ☐   10 − 3 = ☐

8 − 4 = ☐   6 − 2 = ☐   9 − 2 = ☐

Subtract the numbers.

$3 - 2 = \boxed{}$ $2 - 1 = \boxed{}$ $2 - 0 = \boxed{}$

$1 - 1 = \boxed{}$ $3 - 1 = \boxed{}$ $4 - 2 = \boxed{}$

$5 - 4 = \boxed{}$ $5 - 0 = \boxed{}$ $5 - 3 = \boxed{}$

$4 - 1 = \boxed{}$ $4 - 3 = \boxed{}$ $4 - 0 = \boxed{}$

$5 - 2 = \boxed{}$ $4 - 4 = \boxed{}$ $5 - 1 = \boxed{}$

$8 - 5 = \boxed{}$ $9 - 3 = \boxed{}$ $6 - 4 = \boxed{}$

$7 - 4 = \boxed{}$ $6 - 2 = \boxed{}$ $10 - 5 = \boxed{}$

$10 - 2 = \boxed{}$ $7 - 5 = \boxed{}$ $9 - 5 = \boxed{}$

$10 - 3 = \boxed{}$ $8 - 4 = \boxed{}$ $9 - 2 = \boxed{}$

Name

CA CC Content Standards **K.CC.4, K.CC.5, K.OA.1, K.OA.5, K.NBT.1** Mathematical Practices **MP.5, MP.6**

Draw circles to show each number.
Write ten and the extra ones under the circles.
Complete the equations on the bottom.

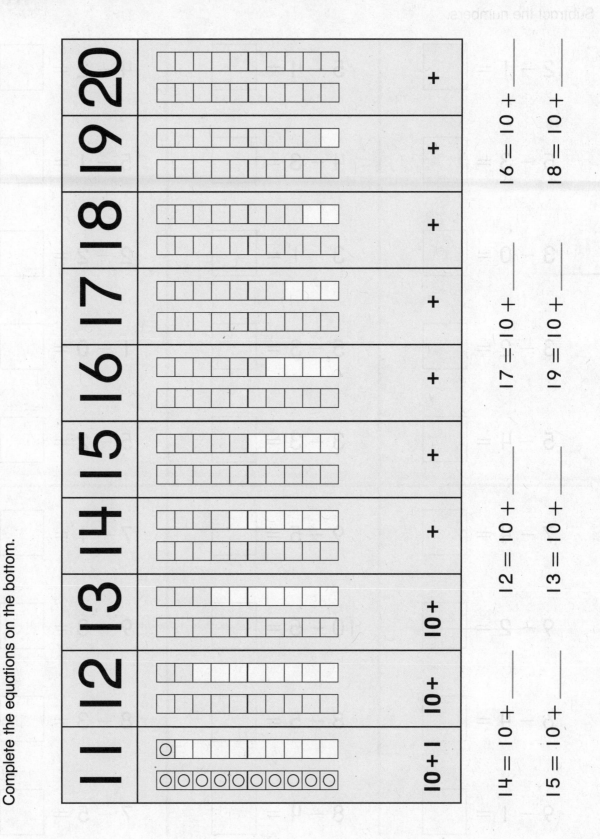

16 = 10 + ___

18 = 10 + ___

17 = 10 + ___

19 = 10 + ___

12 = 10 + ___

13 = 10 + ___

14 = 10 + ___

15 = 10 + ___

Subtract the numbers.

2 − 1 = ☐   5 − 4 = ☐   4 − 2 = ☐

5 − 3 = ☐   4 − 3 = ☐   5 − 1 = ☐

3 − 0 = ☐   3 − 1 = ☐   2 − 2 = ☐

3 − 2 = ☐   5 − 3 = ☐   1 − 0 = ☐

5 − 4 = ☐   3 − 3 = ☐   5 − 2 = ☐

7 − 4 = ☐   9 − 5 = ☐   7 − 1 = ☐

9 − 2 = ☐   10 − 5 = ☐   9 − 3 = ☐

6 − 4 = ☐   8 − 5 = ☐   8 − 3 = ☐

9 − 1 = ☐   8 − 4 = ☐   7 − 5 = ☐

Teen Numbers, Partners, and Equations

Dear Family:

In the next two lessons, your child will be learning how to compare several measurable attributes of objects, including length, height, and weight. They will also learn how to compare the capacity of containers.

Your child will use the words *longer* and *shorter* to compare the lengths of two objects and the words *taller* and *shorter* to compare heights. You can help your child by practicing these comparisons at home. For example, while having a meal, you might ask your child which is taller, the table or the chair. If your child is drawing, you can ask him or her to compare the lengths of two different crayons. Young children have better success comparing length when the two objects are aligned, as shown here.

Your child will also be learning to compare weight and capacity. These comparisons may also be practiced at home. You might ask your child to hold a toy in each hand and say which is *heavier* and which is *lighter*. They will be shown that bigger does not always mean heavier. A pillow, for example, may be lighter than a book that is smaller.

Comparisons of capacity can be practiced at mealtime. You might ask your child to say which holds *more* and which holds *less*, the carton of milk or the drinking glass.

Sincerely,
Your child's teacher

 CA CC

Unit 5 addresses the following standards from the *Common Core State Standards for Mathematics with California Additions*: **K.CC.1, K.CC.2, K.CC.3, K.CC.4, K.CC.4a, K.CC.4c, K.CC.5, K.CC.6, K.CC.7, K.OA.1, K.OA.2, K.OA.3, K.OA.4, K.OA.5, K.NBT.1, K.MD.1, K.MD.2,** and all Mathematical Practices.

Estimada familia:

En las siguientes dos lecciones, su niño aprenderá cómo comparar varios atributos que pueden medirse en los objetos, incluyendo la longitud, la altura y el peso. También aprenderá cómo comparar la capacidad de diferentes recipientes.

Su niño usará los términos *más largo* y *más corto* para comparar la longitud de dos objetos, y los términos *más alto* y *más bajo*, para comparar las alturas. Puede ayudar a su niño practicando estas comparaciones en casa. Por ejemplo, mientras comen, puede preguntarle, cuál es más alta, la mesa o la silla. Si su niño está dibujando, puede pedirle que compare la longitud de dos crayones diferentes. A los niños se les hace más fácil comparar la longitud si los dos objetos que comparan están alineados, como se muestra aquí.

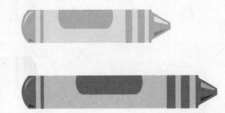

Su niño también aprenderá a comparar peso y capacidad. Estas comparaciones también pueden practicarse en casa. Puede pedirle que sostenga un juguete en cada mano y que diga cuál es *más pesado* y cuál es *más liviano*. Se le enseñará que más grande no siempre quiere decir más pesado. Una almohada, por ejemplo, puede ser más liviana que un libro pequeño.

Las comparaciones de capacidad se pueden practicar a la hora de la comida. Puede pedir a su niño que diga cuál contiene *más* y cuál contiene *menos*, el envase de leche o el vaso.

Atentamente,
El maestro de su niño

 CA CC

En la Unidad 5 se aplican los siguientes estándares auxiliares, contenidos en los *Estándares Estatales Comunes de Matemáticas con Adiciones para California*: **K.CC.1, K.CC.2, K.CC.3, K.CC.4, K.CC.4a, K.CC.4c, K.CC.5, K.CC.6, K.CC.7, K.OA.1, K.OA.2, K.OA.3, K.OA.4, K.OA.5, K.NBT.1, K.MD.1, K.MD.2** y todos los de prácticas matemáticas.

Name _____

CA CC Content Standards **K.CC.3, K.CC.5, K.CC.6, K.CC.7**
Mathematical Practices **MP.2, MP.6, MP.8**

Write the numbers and compare them. Write G for **Greater** and
L for **Less**. Add (draw more) to make the groups **equal**.

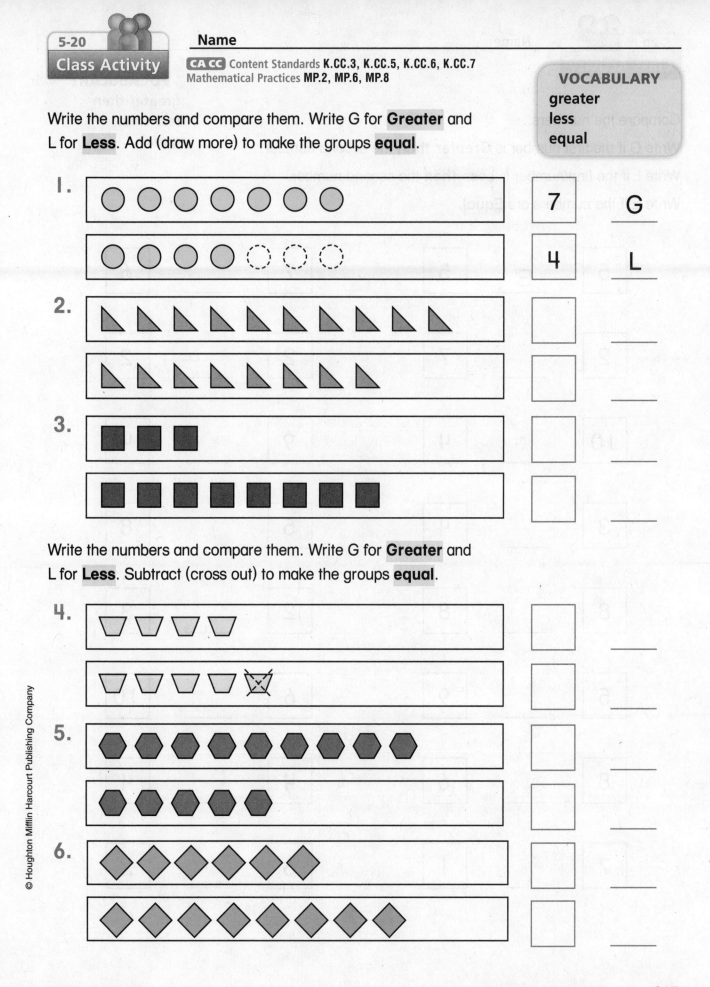

1.

| 7 | G |

| 4 | L |

2.

3.

Write the numbers and compare them. Write G for **Greater** and
L for **Less**. Subtract (cross out) to make the groups **equal**.

4.

5.

6.

© Houghton Mifflin Harcourt Publishing Company

Compare the numbers.

Write G if the first number is **Greater than** the second number.

Write L if the first number is **Less than** the second number.

Write E if the numbers are **Equal**.

> **VOCABULARY**
> greater than
> less than
> equal

5	E	5	7	___	6
2	___	7	2	___	2
10	___	4	9	___	4
3	___	4	5	___	8
8	___	8	2	___	3
5	___	9	6	___	10
8	___	6	4	___	4
7	___	1	6	___	2

Name _____

CA CC Content Standards **K.MD.1, K.MD.2**
Mathematical Practices **MP.2, MP.3, MP.6, MP.7**

Ring the **taller** animal.
Draw a line under the **shorter** animal.

1.

2.

3.

4.

Name

Ring the **longer** fish.
Draw a line under the **shorter** fish.

5.

6.

7.

8.

Focus on Mathematical Practices

Write how many more than ten.
Draw circles to show each teen number.

1. 16 = 10 + _____

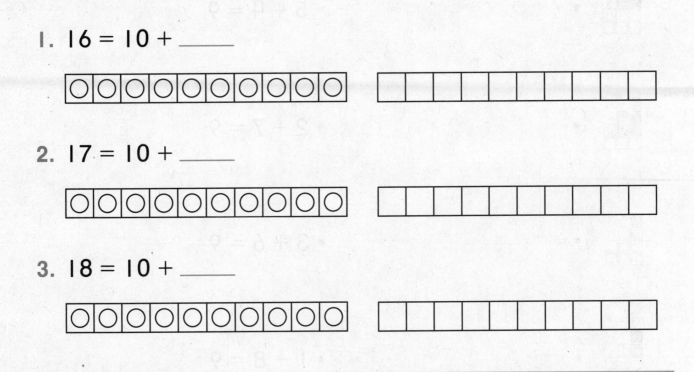

2. 17 = 10 + _____

3. 18 = 10 + _____

Ring the ten ones.
Write the ten ones and more ones in each equation.

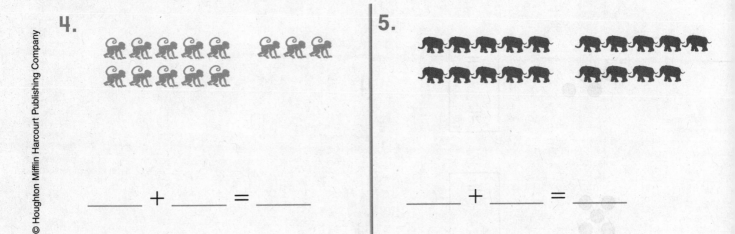

4.

_____ + _____ = _____

5.

_____ + _____ = _____

6. Draw a line to match the picture to the partner equation.

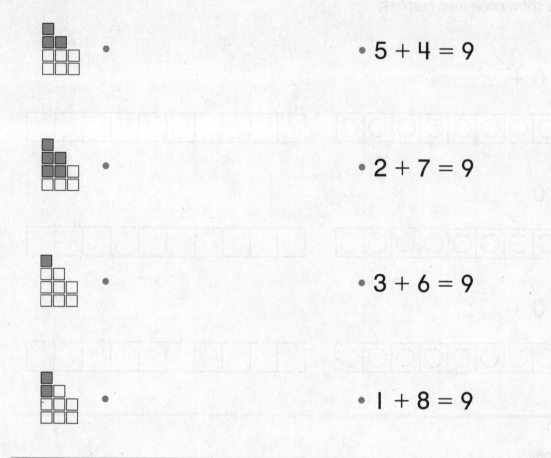

• 5 + 4 = 9

• 2 + 7 = 9

• 3 + 6 = 9

• I + 8 = 9

7. Choose the symbol to show equal or not equal.

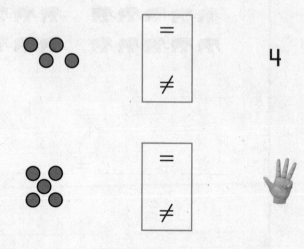

=

≠

4

=

≠

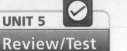
8. Write the numbers and compare them.

Write **G** for **Greater** and **L** for **Less**.

Cross out to make the groups equal.

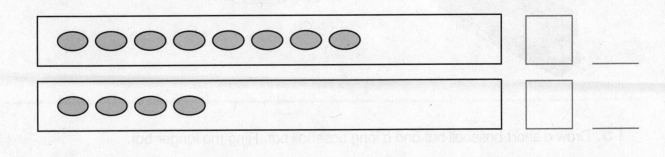

Draw Tiny Tumblers on the Math Mountain and write the partners. Complete the equation.

9.

10.

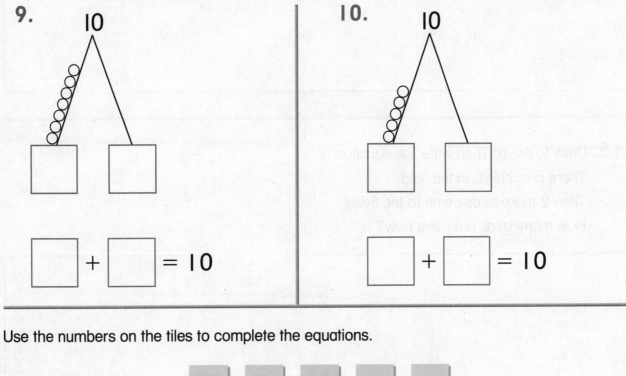

Use the numbers on the tiles to complete the equations.

| 6 | 7 | 8 | 9 | 10 |

11. $10 - 2 = \boxed{}$ **12.** $7 + 2 = \boxed{}$ **13.** $4 + 3 = \boxed{}$

14. Choose the heavier object.

○

○

15. Draw a short baseball bat and a long baseball bat. Ring the longer bat.

16. Draw to solve. Then write the equation.

There are 5 birds in the field.

Then 2 more birds come to the field.

How many birds are there now?

Equation: _____

California Common Core Standards for Mathematical Content

K.CC Counting and Cardinality

Know number names and the count sequence.

K.CC.1	Count to 100 by ones and by tens.	Unit 1 Lesson 17; Unit 2 Lessons 1, 2, 6, 7, 8, 10, 12, 16, 18, 19; Unit 3 Lessons 1, 2, 3; Unit 4 Lessons 12, 15, 16, 17; Unit 5 Lessons 2, 3, 5, 8, 13 **Daily Routine:** Counting Tens and Ones Routine **Quick Practice:** Oral Counting 1–10, Show Fingers 1–10, Giant Number Cards 1–5, Count by Ones from 20 Through 60
K.CC.2	Count forward beginning from a given number within the known sequence (instead of having to begin at 1).	Unit 1 Lesson 7; Unit 2 Lessons 9, 12, 15, 16, 18, 19; Unit 3 Lessons 5, 7, 11; Unit 4 Lesson 15; Unit 5 Lessons 10, 13 **Daily Routine:** Counting Tens and Ones Routine **Quick Practice:** Saying and Showing the 5-Group Pattern, Seeing and Hearing the 5-Group Pattern, The 5-Group Pattern for 6–10, Connect the 5-Group Pattern to Fingers, Count from 10 Through 20 Using Finger Freeze, Say Numbers 11 Through 20 in Order, Count by Ones from 20 Through 60
K.CC.3	Write numbers from 0 to 20. Represent a number of objects with a written numeral 0–20 (with 0 representing a count of no objects).	Unit 1 Lessons 12, 13, 14, 16, 17; Unit 2 Lessons 1, 2, 5, 7, 8, 9, 10, 11, 12, 14, 15, 16, 18, 19; Unit 3 Lessons 1, 4, 5, 6, 7, 11, 12, 13, 14, 18, 19; Unit 4 Lessons 3, 8, 10, 13 16, 18, 20; Unit 5 Lessons 2, 4, 5, 7, 8, 10, 11, 14, 16, 17, 20, 23 **Daily Routine:** Counting Tens and Ones Routine **Quick Practice:** Giant Number Cards 1–5, Giant Number Cards 6–10

Count to tell the number of objects.

K.CC.4a	Understand the relationship between numbers and quantities; connect counting to cardinality. a. When counting objects, say the number names in the standard order, pairing each object with one and only one number name and each number name with one and only one object.	Unit 1 Lessons 1, 2, 3, 4, 5, 6, 7, 8, 9, 11, 12, 13, 14, 15, 16, 17; Unit 2 Lessons 3, 5, 8, 10, 11, 15, 18; Unit 3 Lesson 2; Unit 4 Lessons 1, 3, 12, 16, 20; Unit 5 Lesson 2 **Daily Routine:** Counting Tens and Ones Routine **Quick Practice:** Oral Counting 1–10, Show Fingers 1–10, Giant Number Cards 1–5, Giant Number Cards 6–10

K.CC.4b	Understand the relationship between numbers and quantities; connect counting to cardinality. **b.** Understand that the last number name said tells the number of objects counted. The number of objects is the same regardless of their arrangement or the order in which they were counted.	Unit 1 Lessons 1, 2, 3, 4, 5, 6, 7, 8, 9, 11, 12, 13, 14, 15, 16, 17; Unit 2 Lessons 3, 5, 8, 10, 11, 15; Unit 3 Lessons 2, 11, 15, 18, 19, 20; Unit 4 Lessons 1, 3, 12, 20 **Daily Routine:** Counting Tens and Ones Routine **Quick Practice:** Show Fingers 1–10, Giant Number Cards 1–5, Giant Number Cards 6–10
K.CC.4c	Understand the relationship between numbers and quantities; connect counting to cardinality. **c.** Understand that each successive number name refers to a quantity that is one larger.	Unit 2 Lessons 12, 14, 16, 19; Unit 3 Lessons 5, 7, 11, 12, 13, 14, 20; Unit 4 Lessons 3, 5, 7, 12, 15; Unit 5 Lessons 7, 9, 15, 19, 23 **Daily Routine:** Counting Tens and Ones Routine **Quick Practice:** Oral Counting 1–10, Show Fingers 1–10, Giant Number Cards 1–5, Creative Movement and Sounds
K.CC.5	Count to answer "how many?" questions about as many as 20 things arranged in a line, a rectangular array, or a circle, or as many as 10 things in a scattered configuration; given a number from 1–20, count out that many objects.	Unit 1 Lessons 13, 15, 16; Unit 2 Lessons 1, 2, 3, 4, 5, 7, 8, 9, 10, 12, 14, 15, 16, 18, 20; Unit 3 Lessons 1, 2, 5, 7, 8, 10, 11, 12, 13, 14, 15, 18, 19, 20, 21; Unit 4 Lessons 1, 5, 6, 7, 8, 16; Unit 5 Lessons 1, 2, 3, 4, 7, 14, 15, 16, 17, 19, 20 **Daily Routine:** Counting Tens and Ones Routine **Quick Practice:** Giant Number Cards 1–5, Giant Number Cards 6–10

Compare numbers.

K.CC.6	Identify whether the number of objects in one group is greater than, less than, or equal to the number of objects in another group, e.g., by using matching and counting strategies.	Unit 1 Lessons 9, 11, 12, 13, 15, 16, 17; Unit 2 Lesson 9; Unit 3 Lessons 10, 12; Unit 4 Lessons 6, 10, 20; Unit 5 Lessons 10, 16, 17, 20 **Daily Routine:** Counting Tens and Ones Routine
K.CC.7	Compare two numbers between 1 and 10 presented as written numerals.	Unit 3 Lessons 12, 14; Unit 5 Lessons 10, 16, 17, 20 **Daily Routine:** Counting Tens and Ones Routine

K.OA Operations and Algebraic Thinking

Understand addition as putting together and adding to, and understand subtraction as taking apart and taking from.

K.OA.1	Represent addition and subtraction with objects, fingers, mental images, drawings, sounds (e.g., claps), acting out situations, verbal explanations, expressions, or equations.	Unit 1 Lessons 6, 7, 8, 21; Unit 2 Lessons 2, 3, 5, 6, 7, 9, 10, 11, 12, 14, 15, 16, 19; Unit 3 Lessons 3, 4, 6, 7, 11, 15, 16, 17, 18, 19, 20; Unit 4 Lessons 1, 2, 3, 4, 5, 6, 7, 10, 12, 13, 15, 17, 18, 19, 20; Unit 5 Lessons 3, 4, 6, 7, 8, 10, 12, 13, 14, 15, 16, 18, 19 **Quick Practice:** Practice + 1, Practice + 1 Orally
K.OA.2	Solve addition and subtraction word problems, and add and subtract within 10, e.g., by using objects or drawings to represent the problem.	Unit 1 Lesson 14; Unit 2 Lessons 1, 2, 4, 6, 9, 10, 11, 12, 14, 15, 16, 19; Unit 3 Lessons 1, 3, 4, 7, 11, 16; Unit 4 Lessons 2, 4, 5, 6, 7, 10, 12, 15, 16, 18, 19, 20; Unit 5 Lessons 1, 3, 4, 6, 7, 10, 12, 13, 15, 16, 18, 19
K.OA.3	Decompose numbers less than or equal to 10 into pairs in more than one way, e.g., by using objects or drawings, and record each decomposition by a drawing or equation (e.g., $5 = 2 + 3$ and $5 = 4 + 1$).	Unit 2 Lessons 2, 5, 10, 12, 14, 16, 19, 20; Unit 3 Lessons 3, 4, 6, 16, 17, 18; Unit 4 Lessons 2, 4, 5, 7, 8, 11, 13, 18, 19; Unit 5 Lessons 3, 4, 5, 6, 7, 8, 9, 10, 11, 12, 13, 14, 15, 18
K.OA.4	For any number from 1 to 9, find the number that makes 10 when added to the given number, e.g. by using objects or drawings, and record the answer with a drawing or equation.	Unit 2 Lessons 10, 12, 14, 16, 19; Unit 4 Lessons 2, 4, 8, 11, 13, 18, 19; Unit 5 Lessons 2, 3, 4, 6, 8, 9, 11, 12, 13, 18 **Quick Practice:** The Partner Peek on the 10-Partner Showcase
K.OA.5	Fluently add and subtract within 5.	Unit 2 Lessons 4, 6, 9, 10, 15; Unit 3 Lessons 4, 5, 6, 7, 12, 14, 18, 19; Unit 4 Lessons 3, 12, 15, 16, 17, 18, 20; Unit 5 Lessons 1, 7, 10, 12, 13, 15, 18, 19

K.NBT Number and Operations in Base Ten

Work with numbers 11–19 to gain foundations for place value.

K.NBT.1	Compose and decompose numbers from 11 to 19 into ten ones and some further ones, e.g., by using objects or drawings, and record each composition or decomposition by a drawing or equation (e.g., $18 = 10 + 8$); understand that these numbers are composed of ten ones and one, two, three, four, five, six, seven, eight, or nine ones.	Unit 3 Lessons 2, 3, 5, 6, 8, 13, 15, 17, 18, 19, 20; Unit 4 Lessons 3, 5, 7, 12, 16, 18, 20; Unit 5 Lessons 1, 3, 4, 5, 6, 7, 9, 10, 15, 17, 18, 19, 20, 23 **Quick Practice:** 10 and 1 Make 11…, Show, Say, and See 11–19

K.MD Measurement and Data

Describe and compare measurable attributes.

K.MD.1	Describe measurable attributes of objects, such as length or weight. Describe several measurable attributes of a single object.	Unit 5 Lessons 21, 22, 23
K.MD.2	Directly compare two objects with a measurable attribute in common, to see which object has "more of"/"less of" the attribute, and describe the difference.	Unit 5 Lessons 21, 22, 23

Classify objects and count the number of objects in each category.

K.MD.3	Classify objects into given categories; count the numbers of objects in each category and sort the categories by count.	Unit 1 Lesson 10; Unit 2 Lessons 13, 17, 20; Unit 3 Lessons 10, 12, 21; Unit 4 Lessons 1, 9, 22

K.G Geometry

Identify and describe shapes (squares, circles, triangles, rectangles, hexagons, cubes, cones, cylinders, and spheres).

K.G.1	Describe objects in the environment using names of shapes, and describe the relative positions of these objects using terms such as *above, below, beside, in front of, behind, and next to*.	Unit 1 Lessons 8, 10, 18; Unit 2 Lessons 13, 17, 20: Unit 3 Lessons 10, 12, 21; Unit 4 Lessons 9, 14, 21, 22
K.G.2	Correctly name shapes regardless of their orientations or overall size.	Unit 1 Lessons 8, 10, 18; Unit 2 Lessons 13, 17, 20: Unit 3 Lessons 9, 10, 12, 21; Unit 4 Lessons 9, 14, 21, 22
K.G.3	Identify shapes as two-dimensional (lying in a plane, "flat") or three-dimensional ("solid").	Unit 1 Lessons 8, 10, 18; Unit 4 Lessons 9, 14, 21

Analyze, compare, create, and compose shapes.

K.G.4	Analyze and compare two- and three-dimensional shapes, in different sizes and orientations, using informal language to describe their similarities, differences, parts (e.g., number of sides and vertices/"corners") and other attributes (e.g., having sides of equal length).	Unit 1 Lessons 8, 18; Unit 2 Lessons 13, 17; Unit 3 Lesson 21; Unit 4 Lessons 9, 14, 21, 22
K.G.5	Model shapes in the world by building shapes from components (e.g., sticks and clay balls) and drawing shapes.	Unit 1 Lessons 8, 10, 18; Unit 4 Lessons 9, 21
K.G.6	Compose simple shapes to form larger shapes.	Unit 3 Lesson 9; Unit 4 Lesson 21

California Common Core Standards for Mathematical Practice

MP.1 Make sense of problems and persevere in solving them.

Mathematically proficient students start by explaining to themselves the meaning of a problem and looking for entry points to its solution. They analyze givens, constraints, relationships, and goals. They make conjectures about the form and meaning of the solution and plan a solution pathway rather than simply jumping into a solution attempt. They consider analogous problems, and try special cases and simpler forms of the original problem in order to gain insight into its solution. They monitor and evaluate their progress and change course if necessary. Older students might, depending on the context of the problem, transform algebraic expressions or change the viewing window on their graphing calculator to get the information they need, Mathematically proficient students can explain correspondences between equations, verbal descriptions, tables, and graphs or draw diagrams of important features and relationships, graph data, and search for regularity or trends. Younger students might rely on using concrete objects or pictures to help conceptualize and solve a problem. Mathematically proficient students check their answers to problems using a different method, and they continually ask themselves, "Does this make sense?" They can understand the approaches of others to solving complex problems and identify correspondences between different approaches.

Unit 1 Lessons 8, 9, 10, 18

Unit 2 Lessons 1, 3, 5, 6, 8, 10, 13, 15, 17, 20

Unit 3 Lessons 1, 4, 7, 16, 21

Unit 4 Lessons 2, 3, 4, 5, 6, 9, 10, 12, 14, 15, 21, 22

Unit 5 Lessons 1, 2, 4, 5, 10, 15, 16, 19, 21, 22, 23

MP.2 Reason abstractly and quantitatively.

Mathematically proficient students make sense of quantities and their relationships in problem situations. They bring two complementary abilities to bear on problems involving quantitative relationships: the ability to *decontextualize*—to abstract a given situation and represent it symbolically and manipulate the representing symbols as if they have a life of their own, without necessarily attending to their referents—and the ability to *contextualize*, to pause as needed during the manipulation process in order to probe into the referents for the symbols involved. Quantitative reasoning entails habits of creating a coherent representation of the problem at hand; considering the units involved; attending to the meaning of quantities, not just how to compute them; and knowing and flexibly using different properties of operations and objects.

Unit 1 Lessons 6, 11, 14, 16, 18

Unit 2 Lessons 2, 4, 9, 20

Unit 3 Lessons 1, 3, 4, 10, 11, 12, 14, 21

Unit 4 Lessons 1, 2, 5, 6, 7, 9, 12, 16, 17, 18, 19, 22

Unit 5 Lessons 7, 15, 17, 18, 20, 23

MP.3 Construct viable arguments and critique the reasoning of others.

Mathematically proficient students understand and use stated assumptions, definitions, and previously established results in constructing arguments. They make conjectures and build a logical progression of statements to explore the truth of their conjectures. They are able to analyze situations by breaking them into cases, and can recognize and use counterexamples. They justify their conclusions, communicate them to others, and respond to the arguments of others. They reason inductively about data, making plausible arguments that take into account the context from which the data arose. Mathematically proficient students are also able to compare the effectiveness of two plausible arguments, distinguish correct logic or reasoning from that which is flawed, and—if there is a flaw in an argument—explain what it is. Elementary students can construct arguments using concrete referents such as objects, drawings, diagrams, and actions. Such arguments can make sense and be correct, even though they are not generalized or made formal until later grades. Later, students learn to determine domains to which an argument applies. Students at all grades can listen or read the arguments of others, decide whether they make sense, and ask useful questions to clarify or improve the arguments.

Unit 1 Lessons 4, 6, 10, 15, 18

Unit 2 Lessons 1, 4, 9, 16, 17, 18, 19, 20

Unit 3 Lessons 1, 2, 3, 4, 6, 7, 8, 9, 10, 11, 12, 13, 18, 19, 21

Unit 4 Lessons 1, 8, 9, 11, 13, 14, 17, 19, 21, 22

Unit 5 Lessons 1, 2, 6, 8, 12, 13, 14, 16, 17, 21, 22, 23

MP.4 Model with mathematics.

Mathematically proficient students can apply the mathematics they know to solve problems arising in everyday life, society, and the workplace. In early grades, this might be as simple as writing an addition equation to describe a situation. In middle grades, a student might apply proportional reasoning to plan a school event or analyze a problem in the community. By high school, a student might use geometry to solve a design problem or use a function to describe how one quantity of interest depends on another. Mathematically proficient students who can apply what they know are comfortable making assumptions and approximations to simplify a complicated situation, realizing that these may need revision later. They are able to identify important quantities in a practical situation and map their relationships using such tools as diagrams, two-way tables, graphs, flowcharts and formulas. They can analyze those relationships mathematically to draw conclusions. They routinely interpret their mathematical results in the context of the situation and reflect on whether the results make sense, possibly improving the model if it has not served its purpose.

Unit 1 Lessons 2, 3, 8, 9, 11, 12, 13, 14, 17, 18

Unit 2 Lessons 1, 10, 11, 14, 17, 19, 20

Unit 3 Lessons 1, 4, 7, 21, 21

Unit 4 Lessons 2, 4, 6, 8, 12, 14, 20, 21, 22

Unit 5 Lessons 3, 4, 5, 6, 7, 9, 10, 11, 12, 13, 19, 23

MP.5 Use appropriate tools strategically.

Mathematically proficient students consider the available tools when solving a mathematical problem. These tools might include pencil and paper, concrete models, a ruler, a protractor, a calculator, a spreadsheet, a computer algebra system, a statistical package, or dynamic geometry software. Proficient students are sufficiently familiar with tools appropriate for their grade or course to make sound decisions about when each of these tools might be helpful, recognizing both the insight to be gained and their limitations. For example, mathematically proficient high school students analyze graphs of functions and solutions generated using a graphing calculator. They detect possible errors by strategically using estimation and other mathematical knowledge. When making mathematical models, they know that technology can enable them to visualize the results of varying assumptions, explore consequences, and compare predictions with data. Mathematically proficient students at various grade levels are able to identify relevant external mathematical resources, such as digital content located on a website, and use them to pose or solve problems. They are able to use technological tools to explore and deepen their understanding of concepts.

Unit 1 Lessons, 14, 18

Unit 2 Lessons 4, 9, 19, 20

Unit 3 Lessons 5, 8, 9, 13, 20, 21

Unit 4 Lessons 5, 7, 9, 14, 20, 21, 22

Unit 5 Lessons 5, 6, 10, 19, 23

MP.6 Attend to precision.

Mathematically proficient students try to communicate precisely to others. They try to use clear definitions in discussion with others and in their own reasoning. They state the meaning of the symbols they choose, including using the equal sign consistently and appropriately. They are careful about specifying units of measure, and labeling axes to clarify the correspondence with quantities in a problem. They calculate accurately and efficiently, express numerical answers with a degree of precision appropriate for the problem context. In the elementary grades, students give carefully formulated explanations to each other. By the time they reach high school they have learned to examine claims and make explicit use of definitions.

Unit 1 Lessons 1, 2, 3, 5, 6, 7, 10, 11, 12, 13, 14, 15, 16, 17, 18

Unit 2 Lessons 1, 3, 4, 5, 6, 7, 8, 9, 10, 11, 12, 13, 14, 15, 17, 18, 19, 20

Unit 3 Lessons 1, 2, 3, 4, 5, 6, 8, 9, 10, 11, 12, 13, 14, 15, 17, 19, 20, 21

Unit 4 Lessons 1, 3, 4, 5, 7, 8, 9, 10, 11, 12, 13, 14, 15, 17, 18, 19, 20, 21, 22

Unit 5 Lessons 2, 6, 7, 9, 10, 11, 13, 15, 16, 17, 19, 20, 21, 22, 23

MP.7 Look for and make use of structure.

Mathematically proficient students look closely to discern a pattern or structure. Young students, for example, might notice that three and seven more is the same amount as seven and three more, or they may sort a collection of shapes according to how many sides the shapes have. Later, students will see 7×8 equals the well remembered $7 \times 5 + 7 \times 3$, in preparation for learning about the distributive property. In the expression $x^2 + 9x + 14$, older students can see the 14 as 2×7 and the 9 as $2 + 7$. They recognize the significance of an existing line in a geometric figure and can use the strategy of drawing an auxiliary line for solving problems. They also can step back for an overview and shift perspective. They can see complicated things, such as some algebraic expressions, as single objects or as being composed of several objects. For example, they can see $5 - 3(x - y)^2$ as 5 minus a positive number times a square and use that to realize that its value cannot be more than 5 for any real numbers x and y.

Unit 1 Lessons 1, 4, 5, 6, 7, 8, 9, 10, 17, 18

Unit 2 Lessons 2, 3, 4, 5, 6, 7, 8, 12, 13, 14, 16, 20

Unit 3 Lessons 2, 3, 5, 6, 7, 8, 9, 10, 11, 15, 16, 17, 21

Unit 4 Lessons 1, 2, 4, 5, 6, 7, 8, 9, 11, 12, 13, 14, 15, 16, 20, 21, 22

Unit 5 Lessons 3, 6, 7, 9, 11, 12, 13, 14, 15, 17, 18, 20, 23

MP.8 Look for and express regularity in repeated reasoning.

Mathematically proficient students notice if calculations are repeated, and look both for general methods and for shortcuts. Upper elementary students might notice when dividing 25 by 11 that they are repeating the same calculations over and over again, and conclude they have a repeating decimal. By paying attention to the calculation of slope as they repeatedly check whether points are on the line through (1, 2) with slope 3, middle school students might abstract the equation $(y - 2)/(x - 1) = 3$. Noticing the regularity in the way terms cancel when expanding $(x - 1)(x + 1)$, $(x - 1)(x^2 + x + 1)$, and $(x - 1)(x^3 + x^2 + x + 1)$ might lead them to the general formula for the sum of a geometric series. As they work to solve a problem, mathematically proficient students maintain oversight of the process, while attending to the details. They continually evaluate the reasonableness of their intermediate results.

Unit 1 Lessons 4, 7, 10, 11, 14, 17, 18

Unit 2 Lessons 16, 19, 20

Unit 3 Lessons 4, 5, 6, 7, 8, 9, 10, 12, 13, 14, 15, 17, 18, 19, 20, 21

Unit 4 Lessons 5, 6, 7, 9, 13, 15, 22

Unit 5 Lessons 15, 16, 17, 18, 20, 23

Index

© Houghton Mifflin Harcourt Publishing Company

Index (continued)

Attributes

color, 75, 117, 123, 153–156

compare, 117, 119, 123, 125, 153–156

order, 119, 125

shape, 75, 77, 117, 123, 125, 143, 172, 201, 205–206

size, 75, 117, 119, 123

sort by, 119, 123, 125, 172, 201

B

Break-Apart Numbers, 167–168

Break-Apart Stick, 157–158, 167, 175

C

Centimeter cubes, 29

Circle

describe, 9, 11–12, 171–172

identify and name, 9, 11–12, 143

sort, 11–12, 17–18, 83, 143, 172

Classify

into categories, 75, 117–120, 123–126, 152, 172, 201

and count, 83, 117–120, 123–126, 143

California Common Core Standards.

See California Common Core Standards correlations on the first page of every lesson

Mathematical Content, S1–S4

Mathematical Practices, S5–S8

Compare

by counting, 166, 173, 251, 255–256, 257, 267

fewer, 238

greater, 29, 165–166, 173–174, 255–256, 257–258, 267–268

height, 269

length, 270

less, 165–166, 173–174, 255–256, 257–258, 265–266, 267–268

by matching, 165, 173–174, 185, 199

more, 257, 267

numbers, 32, 79–80, 166, 256

shapes, 11–12, 18, 117, 123, 143, 171–172

Comparing Mat, 13, 29

Cone, 172, 201, 206

describe, 201

identify and name, 201, 206

Content Overview

Unit 1, 1–2, 5–6, 19–20

Unit 2, 41–42

Unit 3, 89–90, 97–98, 101–102, 107–108, 137–138

Unit 4, 149–150, 163–164, 177–178

Unit 5, 211–212, 217–218, 265–266

Corners. *See* Geometry; Vertex/Vertices

Count,

by 1s, 22, 23, 25, 30, 31–32, 33, 43, 47–48, 51–52, 54, 57, 59–60, 63–64, 66, 71–72, 91–92, 95–96,

© Houghton Mifflin Harcourt Publishing Company

179, 183, 187, 189, 215, 222, 223–224, 234

by 10s, 223–224, 234

Cube, 172, 201–202

build, 202

describe, 201

identify and name, 201–202, 205–206

Cylinder, 172, 201, 203

build, 203

describe, 201, 203

identify and name, 201, 205–206

D

Data

classify and count, 83, 117–120, 123–126, 143

sort, 18, 77, 83, 117–120, 123–126, 172, 201

Drawings, math

addition and subtraction, 129, 157–158, 161, 162, 190, 194, 239–244, 255, 257, 259, 263, 267

count, match, and compare, 165–166, 173–174, 199, 238, 251, 255, 257, 267

groups of objects, 7, 25, 31, 51, 57, 59, 63, 66, 71, 121, 127, 131, 239–244

partners, 168, 176, 181, 233, 252, 253

E

Eight. *See also* Partners

groups of, 43, 47–48, 63–64, 91

writing, 63–64, 79

Equal groups, 251, 255, 257, 267

Equal sign (=), 127, 131, 237

Equations. *See* Algebra

F

Family Letter, 1–2, 5–6, 19–20, 41–42, 89–90, 97–98, 101–102, 107–108, 137–138, 149–150, 163–164, 177–178, 211–212, 217–218, 265–266

Five. *See also* Partners

groups of, 7–8, 23, 30, 31, 43, 57, 91, 105, 111, 121, 127, 129–130, 131

writing, 31, 34, 57–58

Five-Counter Strips, 49–50

Five-Square Tiles, 45–46

Fluently within 5. *See* Add; Subtract

Focus on Mathematical Practices, 35–36, 83–84, 143–144, 205–206, 269–270

Four. *See also* Partners

groups of, 7, 25–26, 30, 43

writing, 25–26, 34

© Houghton Mifflin Harcourt Publishing Company

Index (continued)

G

Geometry. *See also* Circle, Cone, Cube, Cylinder, Hexagon, Rectangle, Sphere, Square, Triangle

attributes, 171, 172, 201
  corners, 171
  sides, 35–36, 171

in environment, 69, 84, 205

that roll/don't roll, 201

that stack/don't stack, 201

three-dimensional shapes

attributes of, 172, 201, 205–206
  compare with two-dimensional, 172
  compose, 202, 203
  cone, 172, 201, 206
  cube, 172, 201–202, 205–206
  cylinder, 173, 201–202
  roll, 201
  solid, 172
  sort, 172, 201
  sphere, 172, 205–206
  stack, 201

two-dimensional shapes

circle, 9, 11–12, 18, 22, 35–36, 57, 71, 77, 83–84, 143, 171–172
  combine, 69–70, 113–116
  compare with three-dimensional, 172
  compose, 113–116
  corners, 171
  flat, 172
  hexagon, 73–78, 143–144
  position
    behind, 144
    below, 144
    beside, 144
    next to, 144

rectangle, 15, 18, 25, 35,–36, 63, 77, 83–84, 143–144,171–172
sort, 17–18, 35, 75, 77, 84, 117, 123, 143, 172
square, 15, 17–18, 31, 35–36, 57, 59, 77, 83–84, 143–144, 171–172
trapezoid, 115
triangle, 66, 67, 69–70, 75, 77, 83–84, 113–116, 143–144, 171–172

Groups

comparing, 165–166, 173–174, 199, 238, 251, 255–256, 257, 267

5-group, 105, 111, 121, 127, 129–130, 131

H

Height

compare, 269

Hexagon, 73–78

classify, 75

Hiding Zero Gameboard, 223–228

I

Is not equal to sign (≠), 127, 131, 237

L

Length

compare, 270

O

One

count by, 22, 23, 25, 30, 31–32, 33, 43, 47–48, 51–52, 54, 57, 59–60, 63–64, 66, 71–72, 91–92, 95–96, 179, 183, 187, 189, 215, 222, 223–224, 234

groups of, 43, 91

writing, 21, 34, 58

P

Partners. *See also*; Math Mountain; Tiny Tumblers

of 2, 135

of 3, 135, 191, 195

of 4, 135, 191, 195

of 5, 135, 139, 191, 195, 231

of 6, 136, 139, 191, 195, 235, 260

of 7, 136, 139, 249

of 8, 181, 252, 253

of 9, 252, 253

of 10, 157–158, 167, 175, 191, 195, 247, 260

equations, 191, 195, 219, 260

switched partners, 139, 260

Tiny Tumblers, 168, 176, 181, 233, 252, 253

totals, 253

Path to Fluency, 100, 106, 110, 112, 128, 132, 140, 142, 162, 180, 184, 189, 190, 232, 236, 237, 248, 254, 261

Position words

behind, 144

below, 144

beside, 144

next to, 144

Problem Solving, 27–28, 53, 65

Puzzled Penguin, 8, 29, 44, 62, 80, 81, 92, 122, 130, 141, 152, 190, 196, 216, 256, 258

R

Rectangle, 15–16, 18, 25, 35–36, 63, 77, 83–84, 143–144, 171–172

Represent. *See* Addition; Subtraction

S

Seven. *See also* Partners

groups of, 47–48, 59

writing, 59, 61

Shapes. *See also* Geometry

combine, 69–70, 113–116

flat, 172

position

behind, 144

below, 144

beside, 144

next to, 144

size, 12, 117–118, 123–124

sort by, 17–18, 35, 75, 77, 84, 117–118, 123–124, 143, 172

Six. *See also* Partners

groups of, 47–48, 51–52

writing, 51–52, 61, 80

Sorting

by color, 117–118, 123–124, 153–156

by shape, 17–18, 35, 75, 77, 84, 117–118, 123–124, 143, 172

by size, 117–118, 123–124

Sorting Cards, 117–120, 123–126

Sphere, 172, 201, 205–206

describe, 201

identify and name, 201, 205–206

Square, 15, 17–18, 31, 35–36, 57, 59, 77, 83–84, 143–144, 171–172

Square-Inch Tiles, 3–4

Story Problems, 27–28, 53, 65, 151

Subitizing

perceptual, 23, 30, 47

Subtract

fluency practice, 100, 106, 110, 112, 128, 132, 140, 142, 162, 180, 184, 190, 232, 237, 248, 254, 261

fluently within 5, 100, 106, 110, 112, 128, 132, 140, 142, 162, 180, 184, 190, 232, 237, 248, 254, 261

Subtraction

addition and, 27–28, 53, 65

equations, 100, 106, 110, 112, 128, 132, 140, 142, 162, 180, 184, 190, 196, 232, 237, 248, 254, 261, 262, 264

represent problems, 162

story problems, 27–28, 53, 65

Switched Partners, 139, 260

Symbols

equal sign (=), 45, 55, 127, 131, 237

is not equal to sign (≠), 46, 56, 127, 131, 237

minus sign (−), 46, 56

plus sign (+), 45, 55

=/≠ Tiles, 45–46, 55–56

+/− Tiles, 45–46, 55–56

T

Teen Equation Cards, 159–160

Teen Number Book, 185–186, 193–194, 197–198, 239–244

Teen Numbers, 106, 109, 112, 132, 140, 141–142, 161, 215–216, 220, 221–222, 259, 263

writing, 106, 109, 112, 132, 140, 142

Teen Total Cards, 133–134

Ten. *See also* Partners

count by, 223–224, 234

groups of, 43, 47–48, 71–72, 96, 221, 259

writing, 71–72

Ten-Counter Strips, 93–94

Three. *See also* Partners

groups of, 7, 22, 23, 30

writing, 22, 24, 34

Three-dimensional shapes. *See* Geometry

Tiny Tumblers, 168, 176, 181, 233, 252, 253

Index (continued)

Totals

partners, 253

Triangle, 66, 67, 69–70, 75, 77, 83–84, 113–116, 143–144, 171–172

Two. *See also* Partners

groups of, 7, 23, 30, 57

writing, 21, 34, 57–58

Two-dimensional shapes. *See* Geometry

U

Unit Review and Test, 37–40, 85–88, 145–148, 207–210, 270–274

V

Vertex/Vertices, 171

W

What's the Error?, 8, 29, 44, 62, 80, 81, 92, 122, 130, 141, 152, 190, 196, 216, 256, 258. *See also* Puzzled Penguin

Writing Numbers, 21–22, 24, 25, 31–32, 34, 44, 51–52, 57–58, 59, 61–62, 63–64, 66, 71–72, 79–80, 81–82, 92, 99, 106, 109, 112, 132, 140, 142, 161, 169–170, 181, 223–224, 234, 238, 252

Z

Zero, 32